Counting
Our Blessings

Counting Our Blessings

La Historia
del
Sagrado Corazón de Jesús

A History
of
The Sacred Heart Church
Nambé, New Mexico

Carolina M. Romero de Luján
and
Alfredo Celedón Luján

SUNSTONE PRESS

SANTA FE

Sunstone books may be purchased for educational, business, or sales promotional use.
For information please write: Special Markets Department, Sunstone Press,
P.O. Box 2321, Santa Fe, New Mexico 87504-2321.

Book and Cover design › Vicki Ahl
Body typeface › Times New Roman
Printed on acid-free paper

Library of Congress Cataloging-in-Publication Data

on file

WWW.SUNSTONEPRESS.COM
SUNSTONE PRESS / POST OFFICE BOX 2321 / SANTA FE, NM 87504-2321 /USA
(505) 988-4418 / ORDERS ONLY (800) 243-5644 / FAX (505) 988-1025

Dedicado Con Respeto
Para Nuestros Antepasados
Enseñadores, Enseñadoras

Descansen En Paz

Thanks to many contributions from our parishioners, this second edition of the *Sagrado Corazón de Jesús* church history has some significant revisions. Carolina M. Romero de Luján (Carrie) has made great efforts to secure historical artifacts and solicit *historias de la gente* that accurately reflect the life story of our church—the center of this community—which pulsates metaphorically and spiritually at the heart of Nambé—and is literally situated at the crossroads *de nuestra comunidad.* The church overlooks, like a sentinel, the green *valle* with magnificent views of the blue and crimson Sangre de Cristo Mountains.

The original intent of this document remains intact: to preserve, in writing, *la historia de la iglesia del Sagrado Corazón de Jesús.* In the first edition (1997) we wrote that the church has a rich and colorful history that is impossible to capture entirely in these few pages; this also remains true.

It is also true that many of the names in this book are spelled phonetically, depending on the historical documents from which they were taken. We spelled the names verbatim. Additionally, some respected Spanish editors, who are our friends, have said the correct grammatical positioning of noun-adjective would make the correct name of the church Corazón Sagrado de Jesús; others have said to use the historical name. We've decided to continue with the colloquial church name we've heard all our lives: *El Sagrado Corazón de Jesús*—The Sacred Heart.

In the case of *la gente's* proper names, we had some tough decisions to make. Many names call for an accent mark. Lujan, for example, carries an accent on the a: Luján. However, many of us grew up using our names without the accent mark. For the purposes of this book, we decided to place the accent mark on Lujan, and the same is true of some other names. Depending on the documents from which we took names, we had to make arbitrary decisions about whether to use the accent or not. In many cases we left the accent out, and in others, we included it. The decision rested on whether we consistently saw an accent mark on historical documents. We didn't want to altar common usage while at the same time respecting the grammatical rules as well as contributions we received from parishioners.

Thanks to input from Oliver Maximiliano Rivera, the most significant revision in this second edition is the historical origin of the church. While thorough research was conducted in the first edition, some information was muddled in the transference from historical documents.

Hilario Gomez, with good intentions, had found a photo of Nambé's Church in the archives. In a handwritten account, he asserts: "Original church in Nambé Sagrado Corazón de Jesús … Work started in 1790—church burned down Good Friday 1946." Our assumption is that he obtained this inaccurate information through his research; this is plausible because we, ourselves, have found erroneous "facts" in some documents. For example, *In The Missions of New Mexico Since 1776,* John Kessell writes, in his "NOTES," a reference to *Spanish Mission Churches of New Mexico* by L. Bradford Prince:

> 5. Prince, *Churches*, pp. 301-4. The photograph on p. 302, captioned "Mission Church at Nambé," shows instead the first church of Sagrado Corazón (Sacred Heart) built about 1910 on a hill next to the road from Pojoaque to Chimayó for the non-Indian residents of the Nambé area. It burned in 1946 and was replaced in 1948 by the present heavy "Spanish mission church."

While the year 1910 is apparently correct, the photo is not—it appears to be a picture of a church at Nambé Pueblo. Another specious "fact" in Prince's "Notes" is that the rebuilding of the church was completed in 1948; actually, it was miraculously rebuilt by the community within a year from the day it burned down—it was blessed on March 30, 1947. Needless to say, more work continued after the benediction; this may have confused or misled his research. It, therefore, is likely that the information

Hilario obtained, through no fault of his own, was flawed. Unfortunately, there is no reference to his research other than his handwritten note.

The first edition of this history also stated, "*La Iglesia del Sagrado Corazón de Jesús* was originally built *en* Nambé, *Nuevo México*, in the late 18th Century." This "fact" was taken from a *Santa Fe New Mexican* article, "Fire Destroys Old Nambé Church," found in the state archives, dated April 19, 1946: "State museum authorities said the church was probably of 18th century (sic) origin."

One document submitted by Oliver to Carrie, is a receipt written to his Great Grandfather, Emiterio Rivera, on June 1, 1909, for $10.00 "*de contribución para la capilla*" by *tesorero* Rafael Ortiz. Based on this receipt, we can assume that donations for building the church were being collected in that time frame.

Receipt to Emiterio Rivera by Rafael Ortiz

We appreciate the work of both Hilario Gomez and Oliver Maximiliano Rivera in determining the origin of *The Sagrado Corazón de Jesús* Church in Nambé. It was, in fact, built circa 1910.

As in the first edition, the historical events and vignettes collected in this document were taken from the State of New Mexico Archives and Records Division, the archives of the Archdiocese in Santa Fe, the State Library, and from many interviews conducted by Carrie.

This history has been compiled for the enjoyment and personal records of the beautiful *familias de* Nambé and the surrounding charitable communities that helped rebuild the church. The colloquial narrative voice of this document is intended. It is written in the bilingual northern New Mexican vernacular while being true to the history. Additionally, some of the Spanish translations and spellings are taken from the *Velásquez Spanish Dictionary,* an online Spanish translator, and *A Dictionary of New Mexico & Southern Colorado Spanish*. The "Spanglish" is intentional.

Any omission of events or people is not intended. Any misspellings or typos are *culpa mía*. We made many appeals at church for parishioners to contribute stories, vignettes, family histories, corrections, and revisions to the first edition. To the best of our abilities, we directly or indirectly included every tenable interview, hard copy document, or e-mail that came in. In all likelihood there will be a revision in the future. As in the first edition, "this should be considered a working draft [living document] that will evolve … be modified … edited … and recast as time or necessity changes our church history."

Alfredo Celedón Luján
a *Monarsilla* [*Monaguillo*]
at Nambé's Sagrado Corazón (long ago)
Hijo de Carolina *e* Ismael Ernesto Luján
Nieto de
Nestora Lopez de Luján *y* Celedón
y de Juanita Sena de Romero *y* José Petronilo

Counting Our Blessings

La Iglesia del Sagrado Corazón de Jesús was originally built *en* Nambé, *Nuevo México*, in the early 20th Century. The construction of the original church began circa 1910 and was completed in 1912. It was built on the hill overlooking *el valle*. There is some confusion about who donated the property to the parish. Archdiocese archivists Marina Ochoa and John McMullen found a document that states: *"dos cuadras de tierra fueron donadas por Julian Ortiz, Romolo Luján, José Inez Roybal, José Gaspar Ortiz, y Eliseo Ortiz para levantar la iglesia y para un Cementerio."* It is unclear if the property mentioned is where the existing church and cemetery now are.

The families of the community came together to build the church: los Ortiz, los Romero, los Roybal, los Garduño, los Salazar, los Herrera, los Rivera, los Lopez, los Sandoval, los Maestas, los Gomez, los Valdez, los Gallegos, los Sena, los Garcia, los Trujillo, los Gonzales, los Quintana, los Martinez, los Chavez, and many more helped build our church.

By accident or fate, *la iglesia* was destroyed by fire on Holy Thursday, April 18, 1946. Several parishioners had left the church that day with intentions to return later to adore The Blessed Sacrament. The *veladores* and Sacred Heart *Cofradía* members—José Maria Romero, José Maria Ortiz, Luis Trujillo, Estevan Archuleta, Juan R. Luján, and Alejandrino Romero—had remained at the church. A candle fell on the altar and ignited the fire. *"El Depósito del Monumento del Santísimo,"* fourteen wooden steps covered with white linens that lead to the Tabernacle, was quickly consumed by the flames. Estevan went running to caretaker Sofia Madrid de

Romero's house, where Father Miguel Tallada had gone for a meal and to rest. The Santa Fe Fire Department was summoned. In the meantime, several *Nambeseños* tried to put out the fire with buckets of water, but it was an effort in futility, for the fire was too hot. By the time the fire department arrived, only ashes and adobe remained. According to Esther Gonzales de Romero, the heat was so intense that the bell melted and fell on the ground like a flat tortilla. The melted chalice was also found.

Richard Sandoval's painting of original church

Esther has said that Elizabeth Cable and Mr. and Mrs. John Carrington Woolley donated the existing bell. Also, according to Esther, a tablet was available at the new church that listed the names of all the donors and contributors. That tablet has never been found, but Carrie continues her search for it. "It's probably in some old file," she says.

Soon after the fire, a committee was formed, and it began to plan work and fund raising activities for rebuilding the church. The committee consisted of Seferino Luján, president; Joaquin Ortiz, secretary; Enrique Ortiz, treasurer; Herminio Sandoval; and Frederico Quintana. The committee, along with other parishioners—Estevan Archuleta, Arturo A. Romero, Solomon Luna, and Elvirio Ortiz—initiated the rebuilding project. The committee called on the parish for help.

Eduvigen Valdez funeral at old church

Todas las familias de Nambé y muchos vecinos de la communidad responded and contributed to the renewal of the Sacred Heart. After the rubble from the fire had been cleared, each Nambé family was assigned the responsibility of donating three hundred adobes to the reconstruction project. The adobes were made with *zoquete* from every corner, cranny, *llano, lomita, y nicho de Nambé … arena para los adobes de cada arroyo … paja de cada sombra … agua de cada acequia.*

José Herminio Garcia remembers that when he was a little boy, Pablo Roybal went around with special shaped molds *("formas"/"adoberas")* to surrounding houses in his neighborhood asking people to make adobes that would be used for rebuilding the church. Every parishioner was generous with building material, skill, *espíritu,* labor, prayer, time, money, and especially with faith—even those who were away from Nambé delivered. Luben Espinoza, who was in the military, was always grateful that Luis Ortiz made his share of adobes.

The bond between families, friends, and neighbors was the strength of the community. *La fé de nuestras familias fue la fuerza del proyecto. Cada familia* contributed to the rebuilding efforts. Even before the church burned down, the families worked together to maintain it. Andres Garcia, Sr. said, "*Ya habíamos juntado un dinerito para componer la Iglesia, pero El Sagrado Corazón no quería; él dijo,* 'I want something new.'"

Architect Leo J. Wolgamood was contracted to design the new church. The building contract was awarded to Martin and Ward Construction Company. Herminio Sandoval had been working for this company as a carpenter. Ismael Gonzales and Medardo Ortiz (son of Cesario Ortiz) were the foremen. Enrique Ortiz was first cousin to Medardo. Connections. That's how things got done: *los primos, los amigos, amigas, los camaradas, las hijas, los hijos, los compadres, los nietos, los vecinos*—from near and far—all pitched in.

The actual rebuilding started in July, 1946. Longino Vigil and his father Lorenzo brought cement from Sanbusco's in Santa Fe in Lorenzo's 1939 blue ton and a half *troca.* They brought three loads of the one hundred sacks at a time. "Those were the days when I could pick up a sack with each hand and throw them over my shoulder like they were nothing," Longino says.

The footings were first priority in the project. Some men dug the trenches (there were no backhoes to be seen back then) while others mixed cement or hauled sand and stone. Gilbert Ortiz remembers hauling sand for the church when he was only sixteen years old. Everybody had a job. Some carted water up from the Nambé River. Several peeled *vigas.* Others did upkeep on the church grounds. *Vigas* were trucked from the Jemez dome and Los Alamos.

One can't help but wonder how those heavy *vigas* were transported. It seems like a miracle in itself. Los Alamos was a closed government community back then, so the truck convoy was permitted to go through the city only by escort. The *vigas* were brought down State Road 4 in Santa Fe County trucks (imagine that!) and were unloaded unto the flat bed trucks which were waiting on the west side of the

Rio Grande. The trucks were provided by Lorenzo Vigil, Bernardino Herrera, and Bernardino Romero. Pablo Roybal drove Henry Hoyt's truck. After the *vigas* were transferred to the flat beds, they were taken across the Otowi Bridge, which was very narrow. Don Andres said, "*Si no fuera por Enrique Ortiz,* we would have had a big debt." Enrique had arranged for the use of the County's trucks through Manuel Ortiz, another *primo* who worked for the County, and he volunteered to be a driver himself.

Otowi Bridge, where vigas were crossed over

Hard working men and the horses of Frederico Salazar were used for loading, unloading, and maneuvering the vigas. Ramoncito Romero (son of José Ramon Romero) remembers a story of an incident during an off-loading. The *vigas* had begun sliding off one of the trucks. Without regard for his own safety, Felix Romero jumped between the *vigas* and Silverio Ortiz, who was helping unload them. Felix quickly wedged an iron bar between the *vigas*, stopping them from tumbling off the truck. This act of bravery saved the lives of Silverio and many others who would have been crushed.

There were many other hard workers and contributors to the rebuilding project: Juan Benavidez, Joaquín Garduño, Bernardino Herrera, Celedón Luján, José de La Luz Ortiz, Cesario Ortiz, Edwardo Ortiz, Elizardo Ortiz, Elvirio Ortiz, Arturo A. Romero, Onofre Ortiz, Luis Ortiz, Ramon S. Ortiz, Enrique Romero, Felix Romero, José Ramon Romero, José Petronilo Romero, Rosendo Romero, Vidal Romero, Frederico Salazar, Lorenzo Rivera, Ruebel Rivera, Larkin Salazar, Solomon Luna among many many people from up, down, and beyond the Nambé River—too many to mention.

The younger men of Nambé were also sent to help raise the walls of the church. Ismael "Ernesto" Luján remembers that in September of 1946, he and Mike Ortiz were mixing mud on the southeast side of the church for the men laying the adobes on the southwest side. They had laid adobes up to the window level of the southwest side of the church. An army-recruiting officer who was driving by stopped and asked them if they wanted to enlist. Ernesto looked at Mike and asked if he wanted to join. Mike wasn't sure, so Ernesto asked the recruiting officer to come back in a week. Ernesto says, "He came back in a week. We got in his car and went with him to Santa Fe, and registered." They had done enough volunteer work for the community. Now it was time to serve their country. *¡Qué achaque!*

Church in progress, before it was plastered,
circa 1950

Church in progress continues, visitors:
Seferino Luján and others

Church ready for plaster

Church plastered, 1967.
Photo by Matthew O'Keefe

Gavino Rivera and his brother, Sostenes, originally plastered the inside of the Church. Bids later went out for plastering the walls with cement. José S. Trujillo (Cebolla) won the bid by $15.00. The inside plaster today remains professionally intact, exactly as José did it in late 1946.

Once the walls of the church were up, the roof and the floors were next, of course. *"No más las orillas y el medio faltaban."* Nambé was blessed with carpenters and their skills: José Caralampio Romero, Teofilo Lopez, Procopio (Bob) Romero, Ramon Montoya, Herminio Sandoval, Luben Espinoza, Catalino Ortiz, José Dolores Sandoval, and many others. Gavino Rivera made some of the corbels; the rest were made by Martin and Ward Contractors. A simple altar was built by Luben Espinoza. Teofilo Lopez and Procopio (Bob) made the *graditas* (railings) on the altar, which were removed during Vatican II. They also made the most recent confessional and the stands for Santa Theresita and San José, Santo Niño de Atocha, and Saint Frances of Assisi. Bob, Teofilo, and Luben made the *tarimitas* that are on the altar; they also made the *graditas* on the outside of the choir loft.

First altar showing the chair

There were always problems because the rain and moisture continued to creep through the wood, rotting the *graditas*. They were repaired several times by Gilbert Garduño, Lubin, Abelino Garduño, and Ernesto. Finally, in June 2000, Jesse Vigil, grandson to Longino decided to undertake the project replacing the original wood with redwood. He milled and shaped the *graditas* and installed them; there were never problems with them after that.

The first *matraca* (used for Holy Week) was made by Benigno Romero but was destroyed in the fire. After the rebuilding of the church, a *matraca* was handmade by Arturo A. Because it is no longer used, a photo was taken of the *matraca* and it was returned to Arturo in 2010.

La Matraca/The Wooden Rattle

A handmade dustpan also exists, we don't know who made it; it might have been Benigno, Sofia, Vitalia Valdez de Rivera, or Ramona Lopez de Romero.

Solomon, in an interview with Carrie, said the priest's chair that appears in the picture was later taken to San Antonio church in El Rancho. According to Solomon, he purchased the organ on the choir loft and had it repaired on September 9, 1987. The organ is now downstairs.

Church organ

The altar was made before the pews were put in. The main entrance doors were made and installed by Medardo Ortiz with absolutely no cost to the people. Then the electricians came in to do the wiring. Elvirio was in charge of most of the electrical work of the church until his passing in 1986. Other electricians who were instrumental in wiring the church along with Elvirio were Serafin Roybal, Solomon, and Amadeo Ortiz. Currently, Armando Luján does most of the electrical work.

Altar, Holy Week

Altar showing chandeliers, Holy Week

The two crosses on the towers of the church were made by José Caralampio out of mahogany and were situated in 1959-60 with the help of his son Pedro Nolasco Romero (Pete) and Delfino Romero. According to José Caralampio's wife—Virginia Lopez de Romero—José had just purchased his new equipment for carpentry work. The crosses were one of his first projects. Throughout the years, one of them kept leaning, so it was crooked. It was straightened several times, but it didn't do any good. After the church was re-plastered in 2001, the crosses needed work.

Ernesto was appointed to find someone to fix the tower and the crosses. He was worried because he knew there was no way to fix the tower without tearing off that section of the roof. "Once you tear the roof down, you start having problems with leaks," he said. One night, Ernesto received an answer in his dreams; his revelation was that boards could be used to give the tower more strength without compromising the roof. The crosses have remained straight ever since.

Nambé's *Iglesia del Sagrado Corazón de Jesús* was re-established and ready for its *bendición* within a year from the day it burned down. When finished … "the church was one hundred and twenty-nine feet long and thirty-six feet wide. The height of the towers was twenty-nine feet" (*The Santa Fe New Mexican*, March 31, 1947). It was the fruit of the community's labor. The resurrection of our church was a demonstration of Nambé's strong community along with the help of our neighboring *comunidades*. The church was blessed in March 30, 1947.

The Most Reverend Edwin V. Byrne, Archbishop of Santa Fe, Father Salvadore Gene, Reverend José Llaurado, and Reverend Sigmund Charewicz celebrated the mass and blessing. Two-thousand-five-hundred people attended the ceremony. The congregation consisted of the faithful from Nambé, Nambé Pueblo, Pojoaque, Pojoaque Pueblo, El Rancho, San Ildefonso Pueblo, Española, Santa Clara Pueblo, San Juan Pueblo, Tesuque, Tesuque Pueblo, Santa Fe, Santa Cruz, Chimayo, San Juan, Rio En Medio, Truchas, Rio Chiquito, and other towns and villages. They came on foot, on horseback, wagons, and jalopies. It was a genuine tri-cultural blessing bestowed upon the *Sagrado Corazón de Jesús*.

After the blessing, weekly masses began to be celebrated at our Sacred Heart Church. But even before then, baptisms miraculously took place. The first four children baptized even before the church was re-established were:

David Juanito Garduño	11/17/1946
Adan Delfino Quintana	12/08/1946
Hilario Leroy Ortiz	12/29/1946
Maria Estrella Trujillo	02/23/1947

There were many others, but too many to list here.

The first three marriages after the church was re-established were:

José Medardo Luján and Francisquita Romero	06/01/1947
José Fresquez and Helen Ortiz	09/11/1948
Celedón Gonzales and Dolores Ortiz	02/11/1949

Obviously, there were many marriages after that ... but far too many to list here as well. Naturally, there were many funerals as well. A funeral mass for Atoche Romero in 1950 was celebrated at the Sagrado Corazón de Jesús Church in Nambé followed with a burial at the Santa Fe National Cemetery.

Atoche Romero's funeral

Atoche Romero's interment at
National Cemetery

Needless to say, the Nambé parishioners continued working, praying, and raising funds for the church. The church at this time did not have pews; many of the people took their own chairs, or *tarimitas*, or just stood—and some sat on the floor. Donations continued to pour in. Pews, kneelers, and altars were later made. Heaters were installed. Everyone worked hard. Men, women, and children toiled side by side to raise the walls of Our Sacred Heart once again.

Today, more than half a century after the church burned down, we continue with our devotions, thanks to the generosity *de nuestras familias* who have made tremendous contributions of all kinds, including serving in our ministries and continuing to be custodians of our church—los:

Anaya	Duran	Maestas	Rivera
Archuleta	Espinoza	Martin	Romero
Archibeque	Ewy	Martinez	Roybal
Armenta	Gallegos	Mathieson	Salazar
Baca	Garcia	Mayfield	Sanchez
Barry	Garduño	McCormick	Sandoval
Berry	Giron	McKinney	Skaggs
Benavides	Gomez	Medina	Sena
Benavidez	Gonzales	Melendez	Teel
Briones	Gonzalez	Molina	Trujillo
Cable	Gurduño	Montaño	Ulibarri
Carrino	Hayes	Montoya	Valdez
Carter	Herrera	Mondragon	Vigil
Casados	Hoyt	Mortera	Walsh
Castaneda	Hykel	Nevarez	Woolley
Chaves	Jiron	O'Keefe	Yardman
Chavez	Lopez	Ortiz	
Childers	Lovato	Parish	
Domingues	Luján	Quintana	
Dominguez	Luna	Ribera	

The Mission

The *Iglesia del Sagrado Corazón de Jesús* in Nambé was a mission church out of *Santa Cruz de La Cañada* Parish and was served by priests and assistant priests from Santa Cruz. According to the archives, Deacon John, Arturo A, and Mary Ortiz de Romero, and others interviewed at the same time, the priests who served were Sons of The Holy Family: Reverends Salvadore Gene, Augustine Cortes, José Cubells, Miguel Tallada, José Llamado, Luis Estrada, Frank A. Sierra, Ramon Altimiras, Casimiro Roca, José Ruensa, and Pedro Siguan.

Mary Ortiz de Romero and Arturo A.

After the dedication on March 30, 1947, the priests from Santa Cruz continued serving the Sacred Heart Church until our Most Reverend Edwin V. Byrne decided to establish a new parish at the Sacred Heart Church in Nambé. The new parish would serve Our Lady of Guadalupe in Pojoaque, San Antonio in El Rancho, and San Francisco de Asis in Nambé Pueblo. Reverend Sipio Salas was named pastor of The Sacred Heart Parish in Nambé. He would take his position with the new parish on Sunday, February 1, 1959. In addition, masses were celebrated by Reverend Leo Lucero during this time.

After the Sacred Heart Church became a parish in 1959, a committee consisting of members of the communities of Pojoaque, El Rancho, and Nambé was formed. Edwardo Archuleta, Pablo Roybal, Adelaido Gomez, and Luben Espinoza were some of the first in the committee. Others followed: Lorenzo, Ernesto, Solomon, Estevan, Elvirio, Procopio (Bob), Teodosio Montoya, José Gonzales, Rodolfo Vigil, Edumenio Roybal, T. B. Vigil, Julio Gonzales, and others.

According to Lorenzo, the committee's responsibilities were to be caretakers of the church. The first meeting was held with Father Salas. He lived in Don Emilio's house on *Las Acequias* property. The committee members introduced themselves to Father and told him what needed to be done at Our Lady of Guadalupe Church in Pojoaque. Walls were crumbling, and a lot of work was still needed to be done to finish the Nambé Church.

In the meantime Father Salas was replaced by Father Bernard Senninger on June 30, 1960. Father Senninger said we needed a parish house. He wrote a letter to Archbishop Byrnes recommending the buying of Ernesto Molina's, previously Juan Bautista Rivera's, property. The house and property were bought for $6,000.00.

After the purchase of the house, in July 25, 1960, Pablo was given the responsibility to find someone to remodel it. The contract was given to I.M. Roybal. The Parish House was remodeled and was blessed in May, 1961.

The parish house in Nambé was sold to raise funds for the building of Our Lady of Guadalupe Parish in Pojoaque.

In May, 1961, Reverend Guadalupe Rivera was assigned to the Sacred Heart Parish with plans to find property that would be centralized to better serve the community. In 1965, the parish from Nambé was moved to Our Lady of Guadalupe in Pojoaque, making the Sacred Heart a mission of Our Lady of Guadalupe.

According to a letter from Marina Ochoa, Archivist, dated April 27, 1992, to Rev. Conran Runnebaum, the Sacred Heart continued being listed in the Official Catholic Directory as a parish until 1966 with Our Lady of Guadalupe as one of its missions. Other priests serving Nambé after the parish was moved to Pojoaque have been: The Reverends Arthur Chavez, John C. Rodriguez, Anthony P. Bolman, Tom Zotter, Conran N. Runnebaum, Augustin Moore, and assistant pastors—Ignacio Tafoya, Bruno Radus, John Lanane, Charlie Ortiz, and Jesse Muñoz. It is also very important to note here that Father Alejandro Flores Trejo, from Mexico, said mass at Nambé. Father Trejo would come and stay with Erma Herrera de Luján and her husband Joe and also with Carrie and Ernesto. He thus had permission to serve mass in Nambé.

Blessing of priest's house—May, 1961

Our most recent pastor was Reverend Flavio Santillanes, a philosopher and a wit. He left his home in Lemitar, New Mexico to begin his studies for the priesthood when he was thirteen years old. He studied at Immaculate Heart of Mary High School in Santa Fe. He was sent by Archbishop Michael J. Sheehan to Our Lady of Guadalupe Parish in Pojoaque in 1996. He was celebrating his one month retirement from the U.S. Army, where he had served eighteen years as a military chaplain, retiring as a Lieutenant Colonel. His career as a chaplain took him all over the world. "I love Pojoaque," says Father Santillanes, "I love the quality of the people, the sense of community, and the sense of helpfulness." While in the military, he was out in the field with the soldiers everyday (John Knoll for the *The Santa Fe New Mexican*, June 24, 2001).

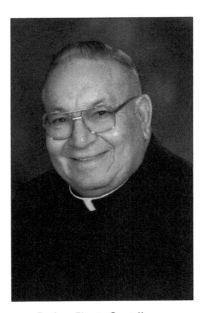

Father Flavio Santillanes

Unfortunately, in the church bulletin dated, February 5, 2012, Father Santillanes announced that he would be retiring on July 31, 2012. He had served the Pojoaque Parish since October 1, 1996. Later, in the church bulletin, dated April 15, 2012, Archbishop Michael J. Sheehan announced that he had appointed Reverend Monsignor Jerome Martinez y Alire, then Rector of St. Francis Cathedral Basilica in Santa Fe, as Pastor of our Parish upon the retirement of Father Santillanes on June 8, 2012. The community feels blessed that Reverend Monsignor Jerome is our present Pastor while at the same time feeling the great loss of Father Santillanes, who served his last mass at the Sacred Heart Church at 8:30 a.m. on June 3, 2012. A reception followed the 10:30 mass in Pojoaque. Approximately 600 parishioners attended. Monsignor Jerome was installed as Pastor of Pojoaque's Nuestra Señora de Guadalupe Parish by Archbishop Michael J. Sheehan on Sunday, June 24, 2012.

Monsignor Jerome Martinez de Alire

Vignettes

Los Pastores
y
Nuestra Señora de Guadalupe

Back in the "olden days," Ramona Lopez de Romero produced two pageants: *Los Pastores* and *Nuestra Señora de Guadalupe.* The pageants were for community entertainment, but they also served as fundraisers for rebuilding the church, especially for getting the pews made and for having them installed. Not only did *Doña* Ramona write and direct the plays, but she also went so far as to make the costumes. She and the cast were transported by school bus to surrounding communities to perform, *mil gracias to* Enrique Ortiz again. They, in fact, raised enough money for the pews. Angela Rivera de Lopez, Fernanda "Fern" Montoya de Giron and many others remember when the pageants were performed at *la sala de la Sociedad Protección Mutua de Trabajadores Unidos* (S.P.M.D.T.U.) and later at the rebuilt church in Nambé. Fern and Angela sat on the then pewless floor to watch those magnificent pageants. Ramoncito Romero, who now resides in Hawaii with his family, remembers that Enrique provided the bus, and Elizardo Ortiz drove it. The troupe traveled to surrounding communities including Chimayo, Española, and Santa Cruz to raise the money. He remembers the last performance was in Nambé's new *Iglesia del Sagrado Corazón de Jesús.*

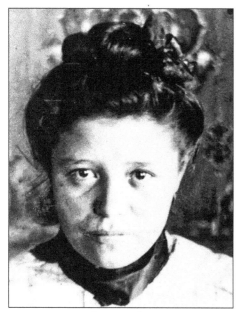

Ramona Lopez de Romero

Ramona Lopez de Romero

The cast for *Los Pastores* was Genoveva Romero de Garduño, who was the Virgin Mary—she was later replaced by Dolores Ortiz de Gonzales. Antonio Garduño was San José until he became ill—he was then replaced by Vidal Romero. Pablito Gomez was San Miguel. The *pastores* were Ramoncito, Arturo Luján, Alberto Luján, Horacio Ortiz, Mariano Garcia, Herminio Garduño, Manuel Herrera, Lazaro Herrera, Sostenes Luján, and Lorenzito Vigil. Arturo A. was San José and the *almitano* (hermit). Elvirio was *bartolo* (rich man). Eliud Ortiz was the *asmodeo* (imp). Estevan was *Satanas* (Satan). Elizardo was the manager. According to an interview with Emily Ortiz de Luján, Fedelina Garduño de Ortiz wrote the verses that were sung behind a curtain during the *Pastores* Pageant. Fedelina, her daughter Emily, and Lucinda Rivera de Sandoval sang.

The cast for the *Nuestra Señora de Guadalupe* pageant was Genoveva Romero de Garduño—again the Virgin (until she got married), then Dolores Ortiz de Gonzales became the virgin; Emily Ortiz de Luján was the angel; the little angels were Shiela Romero de Vigil and Rosalin Ortiz; Nabor Maestas was Juan Diego (*el Indio*), until he passed away. He was then replaced by Arturo A.; Gilberto Garduño was the priest; Elizardo was the *Obispo* (archbishop); Richard Sandoval was Serafin; the *gilas* were Lucille Ortiz de Gonzales and Pita Ortiz.

The accordion music was provided by Ben Luján from El Rancho. One story tells that when Genoveva Romero got married, *Doña* Ramona named Carolina "Carrie" Romero de Luján, her granddaughter, to be the Virgin. Carrie thought that because she was Ramona's granddaughter, she could miss rehearsals. She was wrong. *Doña* Ramona was very stern and quickly replaced Carrie with Dolores. *¡Qué friega!*

Una Poema

The following poem was contributed by Fedelina as she remembers. Fedelina was 92 years old in August, 1996 when she wrote the poem. Fedelina and her husband Eliud lived in Nambé all their lives with their families until he passed away. Fedelina moved to Albuquerque in 1964.

Fedelina Garduño de Ortiz

COMENZAMOS LOS PASTORES

1. *De lugar en lugar*
    porque queríamos pronto
    nuestra Iglesia levantar.

2. *Las gilitas, dos los pastores,*
    seis era San José y María
    un ángel que los quiaba
    y un almitano también.

3. *Era el Diablo y el asmodeo*
    que los andaba rodeando
    para que no creyeran
    lo que estaban mirando.

4. *El Indito y la Indita*
    bailaban con emoción
    para que la pastorela
    cantará con todo su Corazón

5. *La señora que organizó*
    aquí esta pastorela
    que Dios la tenga en la Gloria
    porque era una señora tan Buena.

6. *Aquí les pongo mi nombre*
    con toda mi devoción.
    la madre de las gilas
    su nombre es Fedelina

Los **Pews**

Finally there was enough money to pay for the pews. The contract for making the pews was given to Lalo Lovato from Santa Fe through the efforts of Celedón Luján, who was his *compadre*. Celedón knew of Lalo's carpentry skills. He made the pews complete with kneelers. The kneelers were upholstered by Chuck's Upholstery on March 28, 1996. Ben Valdez, then from Nambé and now from El Rancho, made the book holders. In later years, Ben also made the podium, but when Father Zotter became pastor, he replaced it with a podium that would match the décor; this is according to Ben in an interview on April 18, 2011.

El Altar

The following historical accounts were given by José Gonzales, Pasqual Chavez, Domitilia Garduño de Chavez, Teresita Romero de Sandoval, and Andres, Sr. during many interviews.

Domitilia Garduño de Chavez and Pasqual

Teresita Romero de Sandoval, circa 1930

Teresita Romero de Sandoval, June 28, 2003

Andres Garcia, Sr.

In 1953, a commission was appointed to take charge of finding someone who would make an altar appropriate for the church. The community wanted a really nice and big altar, different from any other. The members of the commission were Eliza Garduño de Gonzales and José, Sabina Gonzales de Herrera and Esperanza, Antonina Sandoval de Garcia and Andres Sr., Teresita and José Dolores, and Domitilia and Pasqual.

On a Sunday after mass, the commission and Father Luis Estrada went in three separate cars to Antonito, Colorado, to visit churches and altars. According to Andres, Jr., Pascual drove his 1956 Buick and Esperanza drove his blue 1953 Nash.

Several churches were visited. The altar they liked best was found in Conejos. The commission brought pictures of the altar to show the people in Nambé. They liked it. The first order of business was to contact local carpenters to see if they could take the contract to make the altar. The carpenters contacted couldn't do it right away, and the community wanted the altar immediately.

The church at Conejos, Colorado

On the third Sunday after the local carpenters were contacted, the commission and Father Luis returned to Antonito, where they contacted Ben Chavez, the carpenter from Antonito who had built the altar in Conejos. Ben agreed to make the altar for $1,200.00 and would come to Nambé to put it up. He said, *"Yo lo hago, ustedes vienen por él, y yo se los pongo allá."* He also recommended that Victor Chavez, a man from Capulin, Colorado, should paint the altar, as he had painted many altars that Ben had made.

Mr. Chavez made the altar in fourteen sections out of plywood. He started to make it in the S.P.M.D.T.U. Hall in Antonito, from an account by Pascual and Domitilia, when he realized he needed more space in which to work. In order to complete the altar, he rented the Golden Nugget Club that was vacant at the time. When he completed the altar, he invited the commission to go see it.

According to Andres Garcia, Jr., his father told him Serafin drove his flat bed one-and-a-half-ton Chevy to pick up the fourteen sections of the altar in Antonito. Carmel Romero's truck was also used. While the altar was being picked up, Antonina and José Gonzales got on scaffolds and painted the front of the church in preparation of the arrival of the altar. Again Enrique came to the rescue by arranging for scaffolds and other equipment needed to complete that project. Ben Chavez came to assemble it, as promised. It took about a week. Some say the community housed Mr. Chavez; others say he stayed in a motel in Pojoaque owned by Amado Ortiz. The altar, as we see it today, was painted by Victor Chavez, as promised.

Mr. and Mrs. Joaquin Ortiz donated the angels on the altar. The Sacred Heart statue on the main altar was donated by Mr. and Mrs. Onofre Ortiz. Mr. and Mrs. Bernardino Herrera donated Santa Theresita in memory of Frank, their son who was a casualty in World War II on May 24, 1945. San José was donated by Mr. and Mrs. Felix Romero. Santo Niño, on the left, was donated by Mr. and Mrs. Elvirio Ortiz. "San Francisco de Asis" was donated by Mr. and Mrs. Solomon Luna in memory of Aurelia Luna de Romero, 1875-1942. Our Blessed Mother was donated by Mr. and Mrs. José Jesús Romero. Also, according to Elida Ortiz, in an interview on May 8, 2012, four gold chalices, one of which is engraved "Donated in Memory of Enrique Salazar, April 31, 1898-June 13, 1989" were donated by the Enrique Salazar family. After the commission paid Mr. Chavez for the completion of the altar, enough money was left to buy "The Last Supper" on the main altar.

The altar of the church at Conejos, Colorado

Sacred Heart statue

Santo Niño

San Fransisco de Asis

Our Blessed Mother

The Last Supper on main altar

In recent years, the processional cross on the altar and its stand were created by Santero Ernesto Rudolfo Luján (Ernie) and donated by Mr. and Mrs. Ernesto Luján in memory of Vidal Romero, Ramona Lopez de Romero, and José Petronilo Romero. The rugs on the floor of the altar were donated by Mr. and Mrs. Ben Luján in memory of Celedón Luján and Nestora Lopez de Luján. The Holy Family, carved by Santero Luisito Luján was donated by Frances Maestas de Montoya.

Processional cross

Rugs on floor of altar

Holy Family

The remodeling of the altar flooring and the two *nichos* on the wall were completed in June, 1995 by contractor James J. Jiron. The carpet on the floor had been torn from wear. The insurance agent recommended that the carpet be repaired or replaced because it was a hazard. Tina Bueno de Herrera, who at the time was financial administrator in charge of buildings and grounds, decided to have the carpeting stripped to expose the beautiful hardwood floors. After consulting with the parish administrators and other parish members, she went ahead with the project. Mr. Jiron was hired to do the work.

Árboles, Arbolitos

y

Arboicilios

Trees in honor of Juanita Sena de Romero's 80th birthday

Two pine trees on the northwest side of the church were donated with monetary contributions by all of Juanita Sena de Romero's grandchildren in honor of her 80th birthday, in June, 1985. The trees were purchased by Ramona Luján de Medina and planted by Robert Castañeda. They have grown nicely and occasionally are decorated for Christmas. One of the trees is shorter than the other because in June 21, 2006, it

45

was discovered that a vehicle, possibly a pickup, went out of control and hit it and the top broke off. We thought the tree was going to die, but thanks again to Longino with his knowledge of trees and with Ernesto's help, the tree survived. It seemed that many people admired the trees and didn't know where they came from, so in 2005, Juanita's grandchildren and great grandchildren again donated money so a memorial plaque could be made. The writing on the plaque was composed by one of Juanita's grandchildren, Alfredo Celedón Luján, and cast by Fred Ortiz from Ortiz Design. Ernesto and another grandson, Ernie, dug the hole for the pole and put it in, Arturo F. Romero made the beautiful wrought iron frame for the plaque and installed it. Longino took his tractor, made a big water retainer around both trees and continues bringing water in his big water tank and waters them as needed. God Bless Longino.

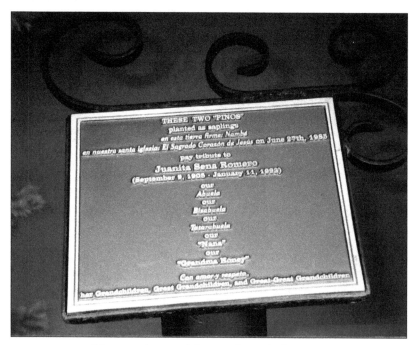

Plaque in honor of Juanita Sena de Romero

Bulto en Nicho

The Sacred Heart *Bulto* enclosed in a *nicho* between the two pine trees was donated by Cordelia Ortiz de Rivera and her husband Lorenzo in memory of Patricio Ortiz—brother to Cordelia. Members of the community have maintained it, as they have done with the rest of the church property.

Sagrado Corazón en nicho before the fire

On Tuesday, May 24, 2011, Arturo A. and his daughter, Cleo Romero, noticed the *nicho* had smoke damage and turned back to investigate. Arturo called Ernesto; Deacon John was notified, in turn the priest was notified by Deacon John. Father Santillanes talked to Ernesto about the situation. At first it appeared that someone had set it on fire deliberately, but after inspection by Ernesto and Longino, who has experience with fires, it was decided that the fire was accidental. They seemed to think that someone may have lit a candle or candles too close to the plastiglass that protected the *bulto*. Because the plastiglass was old and brittle and it was so windy, the assumption is that the fire started by accident. Guillermo Garduño was seen cleaning the smoke damage on the outside of the *nicho* during the week. Ernesto took charge of the restoration project of the *nicho* and the statue of the Sacred Heart. Ernesto, Osmundo Herrera, and David Herrera cleaned the inside of the nicho and white washed the statue. Osmundo painted the statue on June 3. Ernesto and Manuel Martinez plastered the outside of the nicho on June 7. On June 24, Lexan—a better material than plastiglass—was installed by Garcia Glass Co. at a cost to the parish of $439.29.

Nicho after the fire

The parishioners in the community are saddened by the event, but mostly by Guillermo, who has undertaken the responsibility of being the caretaker of the Sacred Heart Statue in the *Nicho*. He makes sure the lamp that Joe L. Martinez installed in front of it is in working order; he puts *farolitos* out at Christmas time and sees that all is working properly.

Nicho after repair/Guillermo Garduño

Stone Sign

The stone sign that appeared on the north side of the Sacred Heart Church along State Road 503 in 2008 is a gift from Robert (Bob) Skaggs and Carl Berny. Initially, this was supposed to be an anonymous donation on their part to beautify the local community. Bob asked permission from Father Santillanes to place the sign on church property just behind the sign that announces the yearly intentions from the Archbishop of Santa Fe. Father Santillanes thought it was a good idea to help beautify and identify the communities, so he approved it. The stone was purchased by Bob from a vendor on the corner of State Road 503 and highway 84/285. The vendor brought it from Villa Nueva, New Mexico. Bob and Carl, with a little help from one of Bob's grandsons, Christopher, carved the letters in the stone, drilled holes in the bottom, created the concrete form, installed two vertical iron bars in the ground and up into the stone, and with the help of Lonny Espinoza placed it in the present location. The stone resides on the border between the Nambé Pueblo reservation and the Pojoaque Pueblo reservation, hence "NAMBÉ" as you are driving east, and "POJOAQUE" as you are driving west. However, the actual boundary between the municipal limits of the two communities is about one mile west of the stone's location.

Nambe and Pojoaque stone sign

In 1970 Leroy Montoya planted the rosebush on the right as you enter the church. Freddie Salazar and Juan Benavidez, Jr. planted the Russian elm trees on the north side of the church. Other bushes were originally planted around the church in the early '70's were bought by the parish and planted by Medardo Luján, José Gonzales, and passers-by who saw the project at work and stopped to help; they were: Carlos Luján, Paul Montoya, and Ponce Luján. Those bushes were voluntarily removed in preparation for the plastering of the church by David Vigil in 2001.

Pojoaque stone sign

David Vigil doing community work

Anthony Archuleta has donated and started replanting some of the trees that had been removed. He planted the pine tree to the right of the church as you enter, he also planted other trees, including the beautiful *alamitos* on the northeast side of the church.

The memorial of the Unborn was donated by the Knights of Columbus. Leonard Garcia, a member of our parish and who is also a Knight, helped put it in.

Memorial for the unborn

El Bathroom

A letter dated June, 1988, from Archbishop Roberto Sanchez to Reverend Tom Zotter grants permission to install a bathroom at the Nambé Church. The Sacred Heart Organization started to raise funds for the project. They raised funds through a raffle and a breakfast. They also received general donations of $1,230.00. A well was drilled on the northeast side of the church, approximately 100 feet from the septic tank at a cost of $3,332.00. Aranda's Plumbing and heating did the gas line for the heater. Aranda provided the commode, lavatory, utility sink, and heater at an estimate cost of $2,698.00. Lorenzo Herrera's account of the work building the bathroom is that the 1,500 gallon septic tank was donated by Montaño Concrete. Robert Romero used his backhoe to open the hole for the septic tank. In later years the septic tank was replaced by a bigger one donated and put in by José Maria Herrera. Benigno Giron made the stall for the commode. Lorenzo and Manuel Tony Archuleta laid the linoleum. Benigno did some plumbing, installing the commode, sink, and hot water heater. He also plastered the walls. Gilbert Garduño did the electrical work.

Donations

Other generous donations for rebuilding the church continued to pour in. Raffles of many items were held: filigree jewelry donated by Basilia Romero de Ortiz; heifers donated by Lorenzo Vigil at different times. Mr. and Mrs. Cyrus McCormick were very generous with their donations, as were Mr. and Mrs. Solomon Luna. Dinners, bake sales, etc. for fund raising were made by the women. Father Salvadore loaned the church $2,000. The $2,000 was used to finish the inside plastering. The priority was to get the church ready for the blessing. The *Nambeseños* continued working raising funds.

Adelicia Ortiz de Luna and Solomon

Contributions have continued. A wrought iron railing for the entrance of the church was made; it was installed and painted by Leroy Montoya. A "Sacred Heart" wooden sign was made by Robert Roybal in 1982 by request of Celine Griego de Ortiz and David who, according to Donaldo Roybal, were *mayordomos* at that time. It has been taken down for cleaning and sanding and repainted by Leonard Lopez and Ernesto. About a week before Easter Sunday in 1998, Anthony Garcia and his young son, Michael were seen painting it again. To see that little boy painting the sign was a joy. Now, years later, the restoration continues.

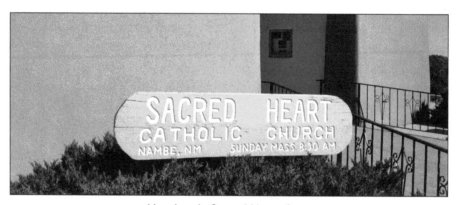

Handmade Sacred Heart Sign

Corpus Christi

Arturo A. remembers his mother, Ramona, telling him the year Corpus Christi first started being celebrated in Nambé was right after *la tormenta del granizo* that destroyed all the crops and killed most of the birds, many small animals, and caused much property damage. That year was called *"El año del granizo."* The people in Nambé made a promise to the Sacred Heart that they would celebrate every Corpus Christi Thursday. This story was told to Arturo A. when he was a child and many more times after that.

In preparation for the Corpus Christi Feast, four altars were always assembled outside of the Sacred Heart church; this photograph was a contribution of Arturo A. The altar was made by Joaquin Ortiz, Cleotilde Salazar de Ortiz, Mary Ortiz de Romero, and Arturo A. in 1959. Carrie also remembers making an altar with Antonina and Adelia Garduño de Benavidez. "We had so much fun. I was very young and learned so much from these two ladies," Carrie says.

One of the last altars made in Nambé before the celebration was moved to Pojoaque

At the feast, a beautiful procession took place with just about everyone in Nambé and the surrounding communities participating. But the Thursday tradition was changed. In a letter dated, June 13, 1959, our Most Reverend Father Edwin V. Byrne asks Father Sipio Salas to arrange to have "… only one large and fervent Corpus Christi procession to be held on the Sunday following the feast. In this way the Catholics of your Parish will be doing what the Catholics of the whole world are doing on that day." Corpus Christi is now celebrated at Our Lady of Guadalupe Parish with five altars made by these societies: The Holy Family, The Sacred Heart Organization, The Altar Society, The Prayer Group, and The Catholic Daughters.

Holy Family

Holy Family in garden

Sacred Heart

Catholic Daughters

Prayer Group

Altar Society

In 2009, during the Corpus Christi Mass, a gust of wind came up, and the statue of Our Sacred Heart was knocked over and shattered. A temporary poster of the Sacred Heart was put up.

Feliz Navidad

Fern tells of her Aunt Lupita Ortiz, better known as Lupe, who in the late 1940's saw a nativity set in a catalog. The set was priced at two dollars and ninety-nine cents ($2.99). Lupe wanted it for the Nambé church. She wanted it so desperately that she went from door to door collecting pennies. With those pennies and more of her own, she collected enough money to order the Nativity set. That set was used at the church during advent until Rose Romero de Olguin donated another one. No one knows what happened to either of those Nativity sets. The one at the church now was brought from Our Lady of Guadalupe Church after Ray Crena donated a beautiful one to Pojoaque in late 1980.

Schools in the Church

Mrs. Cynthia Padilla de Luna's fourth grade class made special Christmas ornaments, such as pine cone angels, glittery snowflakes, felt candy cane horses, and felt mice to adorn the Christmas tree in the Nambé Church. On Sunday, December 20, 1997, at the 8:30 a.m. mass, the children of Mrs. Luna's class presented the ornaments for the offertory. The children remained after mass to decorate the tree with their home-made ornaments. The tree was a beautiful sight!

The children suggested making angels for the tree because they felt that they symbolized Holiness. Pine cones, silk leaves painted gold, and filbert nuts were the materials used in making the angel ornaments. Popsicle sticks painted white and glittered were transformed into snowflakes by gluing them together. Red felt candy cane horses and mice were Mrs. Luna's creations. The children were James Archuleta, Manuel Archuleta, Adam Branch, Jesse Castillo, Alicia Duran, Deborah Duran, Robert Duran, Jessica Garcia, Jeni Griego, Lawrence Hayes, Stephanie Hughes, Alex Martinez, Jenah Martinez, Kimberly Montoya, Casey O'Keefe, Shannon Ortiz, Selina Pacheco, Joseph Romero, Andrea Salazar, Stephanie Sanchez, and David Viarreal.

Las Entradas

In 1995, four upper panels of the main entrance door were removed and the four Archangels in stained glass donated by a friend, Luis Mesa, in memory of Juanita Sena de Romero. They were installed by Ernesto and Alfredo Martinez, Jr.

The fonts at the entrance to the church were donated by Aurelia Sena de Romero and Liberato. A plaque also appeared on the left before you enter the church for the tremendous help by Theresa Bodkin and John Agnew through the Catholic Extension Society of the United States of America. They generously gave donations for the rebuilding of the church. That plaque has been moved to the right along with Nambé

Design plaque, and the plaque donated by the parish in memory of B.J. Gonzales from Rodarte, son to **Ben Gonzales** who made and carved the entrance doors in 2011.

Mayordomos y Mayordomas

After Sofia Madrid de Romero and Benigno purchased their home in 1912, they took it upon themselves to be responsible for the care of the Sacred Heart Church. They also provided a home for meals and rest for the priests that came from Santa Cruz. Benigno was the Sacristan until shortly before his death. They provided the services much like the *mayordomos* of today.

Doors installed by Medardo Ortiz, 1946

The community continues to have *mucho orgullo* in their church. The maintenance of it is done mostly through volunteer work. Also, *mayordomos* are usually four couples, and they see that the church is cleaned and maintained properly. They open and close the church and keep it clean. If any repair work needs to be done, and they cannot do it, they will notify someone who can.

Doña Sofia Madrid de Romero and Benigno

Mil gracias to *Doña* Sofia, Rumalda Romero, and all the other *mayordomas y mayordomos* who throughout the years have kept up the church and grounds. The *mayordomos* in 2011 were Katherine Moore de Romero and Florencio, Jr. (Lench); Nadine Romero de Ulibarri and Eric; Melissa Montaño de Roybal and Fernando; Elaine Romero de Yardman and Donald. On June 15, 2012, Katherine and Florencio were replaced by Florence Salazar de Medina and Ignacio.

In 1987, Sophie Romero de Vigil started taking care of the altar linens and the Blessed Sacrament candle. Soon after, Sophie joined an Environment and Decoration Group. Many times she has decorated the altar with flora found in the natural surroundings. She took care of the altar and decorated for every Sunday celebration and for any other appropriate season.

Melissa Montaño de Roybal and Fernando

Elaine Romero de Yardman and Donald

Nadine Romero de Ulibarri and Eric

Katherine Moore de Romero and Florencio, Jr.

Florence Salazar de Medina
and Ignacio

For Christmas, Longino would buy the Christmas tree and put it up. Both Longino and Sophie and the *mayordomos* and other community members helped them put up the decorations and also bring them down. They did that until the year 2003 when they couldn't do it any longer because of health reasons. Sophie was presented with a Lifetime Membership in the Altar Society. According to Juanita Sandoval de Misere, she started taking care of all the duties that Sophie and Longino did. She also gets Our Blessed Mother ready for all celebrations. Virginia Romero de Martinez, Paula Ortiz de Roybal, and Carolyn Cordova de Romero have helped her with the purificators, *manteles*, and garments. In recent years, Joe L. Martinez has donated an artificial Christmas tree that is used every year for Christmas. Juanita donated the bell on the altar door and also the book holder; Virginia Martinez donated a table that holds the towels, purificators, and gifts.

A Christmas star made out of wrought iron with Christmas lights around it was made by Leroy Montoya in the 1970's. That year he, Virginia Romero de Montoya; Connie Salazar de Valdez and Vianes; and Florinda Medrano de Luján and Armando were *mayordomos*. The star exists; sometimes it's used for Christmas, and sometimes it's not.

Preparaciónes para la Fiesta

Fifty years of the Benediction of the Sacred Heart Church in Nambé was celebrated on June 7, 1997, on *El Día del Sagrado Corazón de Jesús.*

The m*ayordomos* that year decided they would have medallions of the Sacred Heart Church with a very short history written by Alfredo Celedón Luján and engraved in the back by Fred Ortiz Designs. Twenty-seven limited edition were gold laminated; fifty special edition were copper laminated; and the unlimited edition were plain; they all had a turquoise stone embedded. That project netted monies that were put in a trust fund. Projects accomplished with some of that money were the re-furbishing the tin chandeliers—they were repaired by Manuel Aldarete, a tin artist. Three ceiling fans for the church were also purchased and installed by Armando Luján. A plaque was also purchased as a gift to Ralph Ortiz from Ortiz Printing in appreciation for printing the first edition of this history with no cost to the parish or parishioners. The plaque reads:

"IN APPRECIATION FOR THE GENEROUS CONTRIBUTION OF PRINTING
FOR THE 50th ANNIVERSARY OF THE DEDICATION
OF THE SAGRADO CORAZÓN DE JESÚS CHURCH IN NAMBÉ, MAY 24, 1997."

The remainder of the money was used to help pay for the re-plastering of the church. Many thanks to the *mayordomos* who worked so hard selling the medallions and to all the people in the Pojoaque Valley, Española, Santa Fe, and as far as California and Arizona who purchased the medallions. The incoming and outgoing *mayordomos* that year were Claudine Ortiz de Armenta and Larry, Luz Quesada de Lopez and Leonard, Lucille Archuleta de Gonzales and Gilbert, Monica Martinez de Ortiz and Gabriel, Carrie and Ernesto, Sophie and Longino. Also, joining the *mayordomos* as part of the committee were Juan E. Montoya, Harry Montoya, and Deacon John.

If you had gone by the Nambé Church on any day or evening of April or May, 1997, you would have seen a lot of activity in preparation for the celebration of the Golden Anniversary of the Dedication and Blessing of *el Sagrado Corazón de Jesús* church. If you had stopped, you would have seen Luz, Sophie, Lucille, Monica, or Carrie on ladders, stools or even standing on the altar—washing and polishing windows, the altars, *las vigas*, etc. Or you might have found Nestora Roybal de Garduño, Toni Tapia de Romero, her granddaughter Leisha, and Angie Serna de Martinez washing and polishing the pews. You would have found Leonard, Gilbert, Gabriel, and Ernesto cleaning the high *vigas* or painting the back walls. You would have seen Michael Luján, Jr. installing carpet in the back room; José Ramon Archuleta trimming the bushes or painting the black wrought iron railing; Luben Espinoza redoing the railing in front of the church.

An additional *nicho* was made to the right of the porch entrance by Gilbert Garduño and Manuel Martinez. They installed the frame for the opening, where the plaques donated by Ortiz Design, The Fiesta Committee, Theresa Bodkin and John Agnew were placed. A plaque in memory of B. J. Gonzales was also put in that case. He was son to the Ben Gonzales, who installed the new entrance doors and carved them in 2009. He donated the carvings in memory of his son. The plaque was donated by the parish in appreciation for Ben's donation of time and talent.

You might also have seen Matthew J. O'Keefe taking pictures or Larry and Gabriel painting the crosses that José Caralampio installed on the towers of the church. Freddie Salazar might have been picking up some of the church ground trash. Osmundo Herrera would have been touching up the outside paint, or Armando Luján would have been doing electrical work and installing the lights donated by Norma Salazar de Trujillo and Arsenio. The carpet being laid would be from Dominguez Carpet. Gravel and sand was delivered by Los Herreras, Robert Romero, and John Borrego. You would also see Guillermo taking refreshments to the workers.

In preparation for the Nambé celebration, you might have found Deacon John Archuleta, Linda Ortiz de Gonzales, and Barbara Romero de Romero preparing the Liturgy at Our Lady of Guadalupe Church in Pojoaque. Linda might have been coordinating the choirs and the entertainment for the celebration. Deacon John, with Father Flavio Santillanes, might be calling or writing letters to all the priests who had served the Nambé church.

At Pojoaque Middle School you might have found Alfredo preparing drafts of the pamphlet, *"Nuestro Sagrado Corazón de Jesús,"* with the help of his colleague, Thomas Farrell. The pamphlet of the history of the church was distributed after the service.

On the eve of the vespers, June 6, you might find Ben Garcia and his Youth Group and Chic Ortiz setting up a tent for the foods to be served after vespers and at the celebration itself.

On Saturday morning, June 7, at the parish backyard in Pojoaque, you would find the confirmation class of Geraldine Rivera de Dirks decorating. They included Melissa Luján, Miquela Ortiz, Elizabeth Dirks, and Gabriel Roybal. The confirmation class also helped serve. You would find Juan Elizario Montoya preparing food for a luncheon hosted by Father Flavio Santillanes for Archbishop Michael J. Sheehan, visiting priests, and several helpers and the *mayordomos* present.

Geraldine's class

Celebration during 50th Anniversary: L-R: Father Guadalupe Rivera, Longino Vigil, Elizario Montoya, Carrie Luján, and Gabriel Ortiz

Father Rivera, Longino, Elizario, Deacon John, and Sofie Romero de Vigil

Father Santillanes, Deacon John, Luz Quizada de Lopez

Gabriel Ortiz, Leonard Lopez, Luz, Longino, Monica Ortiz, unknown name, and Sofie

Father Conrad Runnabaum, Father Casimiro Roca, Father Rivera, Most Reverend
Michael J. Sheehan, and Father Santillanes

Deacon John Archuleta, Geraldine, Carrie, Kati Montoya de Garcia,
and Deacon Pete Garcia

Saturday was a beautiful day. The celebration of the mass began with the Sacred Heart Cofradía members entering the church, followed by Archbishop Sheehan, Father Santillanes, Father Guadalupe Rivera, Father Anthony J. Bolman, Father Augustin Moore, Father Conran N. Runnabaum, Father Casimiro Roca, Deacons Pete Garcia and John Archuleta.

The celebration of the mass was in honor of the Sacred Heart of Jesús and in memory of our ancestors both living and deceased who contributed to the re-building of the house of God. Father Santillanes welcomed the Archbishop, all the visiting priests, and the congregation. The altar servers were Eric and Aaron Trujillo. There was also a little girl as altar server that we cannot identify. The presentation of the medallions to the Archbishop and the visiting priests present was read by Barbara, and were presented by Carrie. Medallions for Father Zotter, Lucero, Rodriguez, and Salas were delivered to them by Deacon John. A gold medallion was presented to Archbishop Sheehan and to Father Santillanes. A medallion was also delivered to Ralph Ortiz from Ortiz printing for printing the pamphlets at no charge.

Mass ended with a short reading/presentation of the church history by Alfredo and a message from Most Reverend Michael Sheehan. The *Cofradía* sang "Salve Corazón Abierto."

The tent was set up outdoors for food and drink donations. Frances Romero de Montaño and Ramona Luján de Medina were receiving the food donations before mass from many people who were so generous. All of a sudden a gust of wind with rain came. The tarps were flying all over; members of the Sacred Heart *Cofradía* went to help. While mass was being celebrated, the tent went down. It was very quickly decided to serve the food inside the church after mass. By the Grace of God, Gilbert Gonzales had parked his camping trailer next to the tent, and the people out there helped store the food in the trailer until mass was over.

The festivities began after mass. Everyone came together, as usual, and quickly set up tables in the aisle of the church; tablecloths were put on the tables. All the food and drinks were brought in and set on the tables. Individuals that come to mind as being especially helpful were Fernando and Miguel Roybal; Isaac Luján, and the altar servers. Members of Sagrado Corazón Cofradía were helping. What a sight to behold when a community comes together like that. What a wonderful community we live in. May God Bless them all.

Everyone in the present continues to contribute to any project in the church when the help is needed — *como sus antepasados*.

Ventanas en Memoria

All the stained glass windows in the church were donated by individual families in memory of their loved ones, or with special intentions by an organization. The stained glass windows were restored in 2001.

The restoration of the stained glass windows was a big project. The glass had been pitted from the weather elements after so many years. One window at a time was taken down, restored, and replaced. The project was undertaken by Arthur J. Tatkoski from Tatkoski Studios out of Albuquerque. That project alone cost the parish $20,311.50. The project was undertaken in 2001 and completed in 2006. Again, as usual, the community came together to raise funds for this special project. These are the *ventanas en memoria*:

Window in the Choir Loft:

San Miguel Archangel; in memory of José R. Rivera, 1841-1917 and Tomasita Romero 1845-1927; donated by Mr. and Mrs. Herminio Sandoval.

Windows on the left wall of the church as you enter:

Sagrado Corazón de Maria; donated by S.P.M.D.T.U. Concilio #57.

San Isidro; in memory of Cyrus Hall McCormick, 1859-1936; donated by Mr. and Mrs. Cyrus McCormick.

Nuestra Señora de Los Angeles; donated by Lucy Ortiz; in memory of Antonio M. Ortiz, 1863-1915 and Epimenia S. Ortiz, 1869-1942.

Sagrado Corazón de Jesús; donated by Sociedad del Sagrado Corazón.

The door on the northwest side of the church:
Our Blessed Mother; In memory of Nestora Lopez de Luján; 1893-1984; donated by the Ernesto Luján Family
Saint Joseph; In memory of Celedón Luján; 1886-1983; donated by the Ben Luján Family

Window in the Sacristy:
Santa Theresita; In memory of Roman Valdez, 1889-1937, and Teofila R. Valdez 1853–1937

Storage Room to the right of the altar:
La Virgen del Perpeturo Socorro; donated by Mr. and Mrs. Biterbo Quintana.

Windows along the right wall from front to back:
San Antonio; In memory of José I. Roybal; donated by Mrs. José Inez Roybal and Family.

San Francisco; In memory of Francisco Romero, Born Aug. 20, 1922 – Died, June 12, 1944, U.S. Army Marignay Manghe, France; donated by José Ascension Romero.

Sagrada Familia; donated by Mr. and Mrs. Pablo Sena.

San José; In memory of Noverta L. Gonzales, 1864-1942; donated by Belarmino and Bernardita Gonzales.

Renovation Project for Outside of the Church

The Youth Group made an announcement that a Thanksgiving Turkey Bingo would take place on Saturday, November 17, 2001 and that all proceeds would be donated for the Nambé Church Repair. I repeat—what a great community we live in!

On May 21, 2009, Deacon John called an informal meeting at the *Iglesia del Sagrado Corazón de Jesús* in Nambé. In attendance were Lorenzo, Arturo F. Romero, Carrie and Ernesto, Juanita, Paula, Longino and Sophie, Guillermo, Karl Gonzales, and Oliver. The meeting was to explain what needed to be done to the church. A renovation project was put in place to plaster the church, to install a handicap ramp, to have new doors made for both the main entrance and the priests' entrance on the northwest side, and to fix the slope on the west side of the church.

Meeting for Church in Progress, 2009: Guillermo Garduño, Karl K. Gonzales, Deacon John Archuleta, Lorenzo Herrera, Longino Vigil, Ernesto Luján, Arturo F. Romero, and Oliver Rivera

Again, the people of the community got together and donated monies in memory of their loved ones. The remainder of the money from the medallion sales from the 50th celebration was also used for this project. In addition, $5000.00 bequeathed by Rose Romero de Olguin, was used for the renovation of the outside of the church.

New doors were constructed by Benedict J. Gonzales, carpenter from Ribera, New Mexico. Mr. Gonzales carefully removed the stained glass archangels from old doors and replaced them on the new entrance door. The Sacred Heart carvings on the doors were created by him in memory of his son B. J. without charge to the parish. B.J. had been killed in an automobile accident on I-25 between Las Vegas and Santa Fe at mile marker 326. He had just graduated from West Las Vegas High School and was working with his dad doing carpentry work that they both loved to do. He had also attended seventh to tenth grade at Pecos. Mr. Gonzales and his family have also started a Memorial Scholarship for B.J. at the Pecos and West Las Vegas Schools. The doors were completed and put up on March 12, 2010. Mr. Gonzales also made the doors for the northwest entrance. He installed the stained glass windows of Our Blessed Mother and Saint Joseph—these stained glass windows were made by Julian Mesa of Jugo Mesa Studios, Tarpon Springs, Florida—brother of Luis Mesa—who had made the stained glass windows of the archangels for the entrance door seventeen years earlier. A memorial and dedication of the doors took place on May 22, 2011 after the 8:30 a.m. mass. In attendance were Ben, his wife Molly; their daughter Alicia; Deacon John, and the congregation; the blessing was conducted by Father Santillanes.

Installation of new doors

Installation of doors

Entrance door carved by Benedict J. Gonzales

Doors on west side with stained glass of Blessed Mother and St. Joseph, made and installed Benedict J. Gonzales

After the planning committee decided what needed to be done, Ronnie Duran from New Mexico Construction and Floor Systems, Inc. from El Rancho was contacted and advised on what needed to be done. He and Carlos Ortiz came to check the roof and the rest of the church out. Mr. Duran submitted a proposal to the church and to the Archdiocese. The proposal was approved by Marina Ochoa. After completion of the projects, Marina congratulated Mr. Duran for a job well done.

The project was begun. Some of the work was subcontracted to others according to Ronnie. On the west side of the church, the sidewalk and handicap entrance along with the porch, and the paving, gravel and bumpers were also done by Ronnie and his helpers Arnold Jaquez and José Griego. The wrought iron railing on the west side of the church was made by Anthony Montoya, also from El Rancho. The inside of the church was also worked on. The walls were painted. The *vigas* were cleaned and refinished, and the floors were sanded and refinished as well.

Anthony Montoya and wrought iron railing

Wrought iron railing

All the above work was done and completed about the same time the doors were done in 2010.

Plastering of the Outside of the Church

The outside walls of the church were in dire need of repair. It was decided to re-plaster. The job was given to Duran Enterprises, CPI Contractors. A letter from Mr. Gilbert Duran was submitted to the parish office explaining what all had to be done to prepare the wall for proper plastering and the procedures that needed to be done. He explained that after the year 1950, cement plaster replaced traditional mud and lime plaster to a large extent. Cement is less permeable than softer materials and tends to trap water within the walls. Because cement plaster is rigid and not compatible with softer adobe material, it will tend to crack. These cracks allow water to penetrate walls, so, in order to do a good job, the wall had to be power washed because of the paint, existing stucco had to be removed in three areas and new 17 gauge stucco mesh had to be applied with mechanical fasteners and a scratch and leveling coat power wash and recoat entire area with synthetic finish that had to be applied to entire surface. Mr. Duran donated most of the materials. The cost of the project only cost the parish $20,000.00. If the parish had paid full price, it would have cost $80,000.00 to $100,000.00. Mr. Duran made a most generous contribution. The following are some of the crew members working on the project: Joe Sandoval, Lorenzo Carrillos, Joseph Fernandez, Richard Romero, Joey Sandoval, Manuel Baca, Cosmos Terajas, Baltazar Balcirta, Anthony Romero, and George Diaz.

Church before plastering, 2001

Another angle of church before plastering, 2001

Scaffolds before plastering begins

Father Santillanes before plastering begins

Plasterers

Plastering in progress

Almost finished with the
plastering

Plastering job completed

The plastering was completed in February, 2001. A plaque was presented to Mr. and Mrs. Gilbert Duran in appreciation of their great contribution to the church.

The Roof

The repair of the church roof was subcontracted. Mr. Ronnie Duran fixed the roof for the last time in 2010. It had been repaired many times before but had continued leaking. Originally, from an account by Magdalena Gonzales de Ortiz, her husband,

Ramon S. Ortiz, had told her when the original roof was put on the building in 1946, it had no slope. They later tried to install a slope but couldn't do it more successfully.

A letter from Pojoaque architect Allen McNown, written on March 3, 1979, says the original roof was mopped with tar and gravel. The roof was installed over pine decking over pine *vigas*. When installed, it only had a slope of about eight inches; therefore, it was almost level. According to available records, the roof was fixed in 1974 by Librado Herrera, and again in 1979 by Andy's Roofing Service, and again in 1995 by Los Alamos Roofing, Inc. Duran Enterprises de Santa Fe, Inc. undertook the job of fixing the leaking roof yet again. Insulation was put in. Also, one of the leaking problems at this time was three lintels and/or *canales* (rain spouts) made of wood had rotted. That problem was resolved. The roof was fixed again! It hasn't leaked since.

The Floors

As long as the roof continued leaking, the *vigas* continued getting stained, and the floor continued getting warped, and work needed to be done over and over. In 1995, Robert Duran contracted to redo the floor of the church. The community again came together and moved all the pews from the church to the S.P.M.D.T.U. Hall. A thorough job was done on the floor. When it was complete, the same *ayudantes* took the pews back and put them in place.

Doblando

Two bells exist in the tower of the church. One is for regular ringing; the other is to toll (*doblar*). When a person in the community passed away in the olden days, the only way of communicating the loss to the community was by ringing/tolling the bell. One toll with a pause for each year of a woman's age and two tolls with a pause in between for the age of a man. Not many churches still use that tradition.

Monarsillas (Altar Boys) – Altar Servers

The only person who remembers being an altar boy before the old church burned down is Manuel Romero—then from Nambé and now from Santa Fe. Manuel remembers the wall at the altar being sky blue and the only other thing he remembers is a black pot belly stove. Manuel also remembers that in those days individual families rented their own pews. Many times in those days the priests from Santa Cruz de La Cañada used to bring their own altar boys.

After the church burned down and was re-built, the altar boys in the mid-fifties and early sixties were: Ben Luján, Ponce Luján, John Archuleta, Miguel Luján, David Ortiz, Gilbert (Gillie) Ortiz, Serafin (Finnie) Roybal, Ramos Vigil, Robert Vigil, Joe Vigil, Don Roybal, Alfredo Luján, Alfredo Martinez Jr., Anthony Ortiz, Ernesto R. Luján (Ernie), Rick Romero, Alex Martinez, Ronnie Martinez, and Gilbert Rivera. There were many more, but these are the only names that have surfaced to this point. Others in the late '90's have been Aaron and Eric Trujillo.

Only boys served in the early days. In later years after Vatican II, girls were also allowed to serve, so the name was changed to Altar Servers. Throughout the years, other altar servers in Nambé have been Joseph Romero, Andres Sanchez, Diego Sanchez, David Roybal, Sam Roybal, Nicholas Ortiz, Dylan Merrigan, Maggie Merrigan, Lizzie Merrigan, Rachel Roybal, Lillie Parish, Mychael Parish, Noah Simpson, James Garcia, Gabriel Montoya, Adrianna Quintana, Theresa Roybal, Andrew Roybal, James Roybal, James Garcia, Tia Roybal, Ernie Vigil, Nicolette Martinez, Matthew Quintana, Matthew Martinez, Tomas Teel, Francesca Martinez, Francine Martinez. The altar servers in Nambé most recently have been Lauren Armenta, Lawrence Armenta, Katlyn Yardman, JenniferYardman, and Jacob DeVargas.

Volunteer Leadership Roles in the Church

Acolytes

Acolytes assist the priest in the celebration of the mass.

In addition to Sean Ewy, who has long been an acolyte, eight more were installed on November 25, 2012, at the 10:30 mass:

Nicholas Garcia

Gary Johnson

Gerard Martinez

Marty Martinez

Mike Martinez

Harry Montoya

Greg Romero

Donald Yardman

Deacons, Lectors, and Ministers

The extraordinary ministers assist the priest and the deacons. The Deacons are Ordained Clergy who have received the Sacrament of The Holy Orders. The Deacons who continue to serve the parish to this day are Deacon Pete Garcia, Deacon John Archuleta, Deacon Rueben Roybal, and Deacon Dan Valdez.

Benigno Romero served as Sacristan (one in charge of Sacred Vessels) in the old church before it burned down. Today Ophelia Romero has taken that ministry.

The Eucharistic Ministers are Consuelo Martinez de Dominguez, Loyola Roybal de Trujillo, Virgina Romero de Martinez, Norma Garcia de Valdez, Clara Salazar de Briones, Ophelia, Tina, Stephanie Sanchez de Mortera, and Matthew Hykel.

The Lectors are Celine, David, Michael Montoya, Orlinda Ortiz de Roybal, Lou Mortera, Monica Gonzales de Roybal, Barbara Romero, and Stephanie.

El Coro

According to an account by Fern from an interview with Avelina Rivera de Montoya and with Frances Romero de Luján on April 2012, in the late thirties before the old church burned down, a lady named Gregoria came with the priests from Santa Cruz de La Cañada Parish to sing requiem masses. Also, around that time, Luisita Quintana came from Santa Fe to sing Christmas Eve mass every Christmas Eve for many years. She was a relative of Antonia and Amarante Quintana from Pojoaque.

In the 1940s, Cordelia assembled a choir. She had most of the elementary school girls participating. Among them were Polly Ortiz de Trujillo, Carrie, Lydia Romero de McBride, Jennie Ortiz de Rowlison, Angie Ortiz de Hayes, Lorraine Romero de Montoya, Annabelle Sandoval, Mela Garduño de Lucero, Fabiola Garduño de Lucero, Nestora, Gloria Rivera de Gould, Candelaria (Candy) Gomez, Miquella Herrera, and many others. In later years, Cordelia, along with Frances continued leading the choir. Maria Casias, a nurse at the Nambé school, played the organ and also sang for many years.

When Cordelia was unable to lead the choir any longer, Frances continued until many years after that with Christina Rivera de Hyde playing the organ. Joe Salazar was choir director in the fifties. A choir was started by David Ortiz and handed over to Fern in the middle 70's. She directed that choir for eighteen years. Florencio

Romero had a choir for seven years. Annabelle Lopez de Rivera directed the choir in the early 2000s for five years. Juanita directed the choir for six years after that. Also by accounts from Fern, others that have sang in the choirs throughout the years have been Angela, Avelina, Betty Rivera de Valencia, Corine Rivera de Madrid, Geraldine, Sylvia Ortiz de Hoover, Bertha Rivera de Gallegos, Elaine Quintana de Baca, Susie Maes de Montoya, Margie Rivera de Roybal, Mary Roybal, Ramona Roybal de Gonzales, Bertha Castillo de Montoya, Norma, Josie Romero de Pacheco, Virginia Romero de Montoya, Angie Serna de Martinez, Virginia Romero de Martinez, Marlene Romero de Luján, Patricia Tapia de Gomez, Florinda, Vicenta Ortiz de Luján, Toni, Pablo Romero, Mario Romero, Michael Montoya, Jerry Romero, Grace Valdez de Romero, Lou Martinez de Valdez, Celine, Patty Brewer de Romero, Fermina Garduño de Valdez, Refufito(Ruth) Sandoval de Jiron, Agneda Valdez de Trujillo, Ambrosia Valdez de Hutt, Rafaelita Lopez de Martinez, Annabelle Romero de Pando, Linda, Patricia Luján de Quintana, Lourdes Rivera, Veronica Rivera de Schroer, Carmen Romero de Herrera, Barbara Romero de Alba, Victoria Tapia, Edwin Tapia, Regina Romero and daughter Arica, Tommy Sisneros, Wilfred Romero, Charlie Luján, Armando Luján, Danny Ortiz, Robert Romero, and Chris Martinez. Renae Gonzales de Lopez has been singing once a month for twenty-four years.

Palm Sunday, April 1, 2012, a choir put together by Lawrence Herrera, consisting of Charles Luján, Lawrence, Ronnie, and Gilbert Estrada sang the mass. According to Lawrence they will try to become members of the choir community. On the first Sunday of the month, *La Sociedad del Sagrado Corazón de Jesús* leads the congregation in song with "Salve Corazón Abierto," "Cantico de Maria," "Sagrado Corazón de Jesús," and whatever hymn is appropriate. On special occasions, such as the Celebration of The Sacred Heart, other choirs have come to lead the congregation. They are Margarita Bustos de Trujillo choir, Wilfred with the Ortiz sisters, Wilfred with the Martinez brothers, The ACTS Choir which consists of Thomas Montaño, Larry Herrera, Lawrence, Gilbert, Florean Lucero, Thomas Zamora, Phillip Trujillo, and others.

Los Ushers

At one time or another, it seems every man in the community has served as usher. In the late 1980's Manuel Antonio (Tony) Archuleta was put in charge of the ushers. He compiled a list of the ushers. He kept the list with dates and telephone numbers. He would call each member whose turn it was to usher on Saturday evenings to remind them. When Tony passed away in 1992, Deacon Pete Garcia continued the practice. Soon after that Father Conran sent a letter to Ernesto asking him if he would continue that ministry. Ernesto, along with Carrie, continue with the list and phone numbers. They have never found it necessary to call anyone to remind them. If a designated usher is absent, there is always someone there willing to step in. They update the list every January of the new year. Ushers are no longer just men; women also participate. Some of the ushers throughout the years have been Oliver Rivera, Arturo F., Joe L., Michael Roybal, Alfred Roybal, David, Celine, Jerry Garcia, Andres Jr., Arsenio, Vincent Nasca, Karl Gonzales, Rick Romero, Ben Luján, Longino Vigil, Ernesto, Alfredo, Jerome Luján, Joseph Luján, Pablo Gonzales, Minnie Perez de Walsh, Gilbert Estrada, Gene Montoya, Lawrence Herrera, Joe Trujillo, Joey Trujillo, Guillermo, Joshua Trujillo, Arturo A., Lorenzo Herrera, Orlando Ortiz, and many others.

Flags on the Altar

A United States Flag on the altar was donated by Andres Garcia, Jr. in memory of his father, Andres Garcia, Sr. Andres, Jr. had gone to another church and noticed a flag there. He thought it was appropriate to donate one to the church since his father was a World War II veteran, and Andres, Jr. is a Korean war veteran. Father Santillanes gave him permission to present it at the celebration of the Sacred Heart in June, 2003. A State of New Mexico flag was presented by David Ortiz in June 2007, also on the celebration of the Sacred Heart; it was donated by Melvin Chavez, President of

Lodge 3 of the Woodmen of the World, Santa Fe, New Mexico. The Woodmen of the World is a fraternal insurance society that presents flags to schools, churches, and other nonprofit organizations.

United States Flag on altar

New Mexico Flag on altar

Elida also said that Petrita Vigil de Romero had said that the Stations of The Cross were purchased by the people in the community.

A tin frame for the photograph of Pope Benedict XVI was made and donated by an award winning Santera, Cleo Romero, in June, 2010. Also, Jorge Trujillo, son of José Cebolla, made a tin frame, inserted into it a picture of The Divine Mercy, and donated it to the church.

Tin Frame and photo of
Pope Benedict XVI with
the Sacred Heart

Tin Frame and photo
of Divine Mercy

La Union Del Sagrado Corazón de Jesús Concilio
(Catholic Union of the Sacred Heart of Jesús)

La Sociedad del Sagrado Corazón de Jesús (The Catholic Union of the Sacred
Heart of Jesús) was formed in Pojoaque, New Mexico on Sunday, May 1, 1916.

The society consists of a director (the parish priest), a president, vice-president,
secretary, treasurer, and sergeant-at-arms. The officials are elected annually. The
purpose of the organization is to promote the welfare of families, promote Christian
faith to our youth, for the help of the poor and needy, to help the sick, to bury the dead,
and to comfort the families. Members from surrounding communities were called
"Linderos"; they would come on horseback or they would walk to the meetings. We
are fortunate to have a copy of the original receipt that includes the names of the first
officers of *La Sociedad*. The members of the organization on May 1, 1916 were:

Benigno Romero	José de la Luz Sandoval	Juan B. Rivera	Valentin Valdez
Todocio Ortiz	Teodoro Trujillo	Esquipula Montoya	Navor Mestas
Lorenzo Romero	José M. Ortiz	E. Salazar y Garcia	Relles Trujillo
José A. Luján	Sotero Martinez	José Antonio Salazar	Antonio M. Ortiz
Ramon S. Trujillo	Genaro Quintana	José Angel Romero	Ramon R. Rodarte
Antonio E. Romero	E. Salazar y Trujillo	Antonio Roybal	Alfredo Garcia
Evaristo Trujillo	Silverio Garcia	Manuel S. Roybal	Severo Sena
Francito Chavez	Eutimio Roybal	José P. Quintana	Hilario Calle
Cosme Garcia			

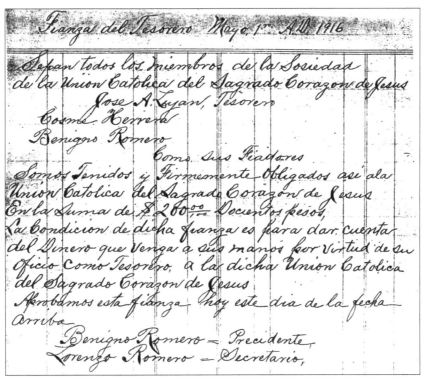

Fianza del Tesorero Mayo 1, A.D. 1916

The organization owned its own meeting place, a house in Pojoaque. When funds were being raised for the building of Our Lady of Guadalupe church in Pojoaque, Pablo Roybal, who was the president at that time, suggested to the members that the house be sold to raise funds for that purpose. It was approved and sold. It was promised to them that a room at the Parish Hall would always be available for their monthly meetings that are held the first Sunday of every month. For some reason or for the inconvenience of going to Pojoaque, the society holds their meetings after the 8:30 a.m. mass in the church in Nambé. Every time a secretary was elected, the records went along with him to his home. At one of their monthly meetings it was decided that, with permission from the parish priest, a storage place could be built on the choir loft to store their records. Benito Valdez built a storage room with a door and lock to safeguard the records. That storage room also contains a big trunk that holds all the artifacts for which Carrie still hopes someone will make a display case. It also holds the linens and decorations owned and used by the Society for the Corpus Christi altar.

Artifacts in storage

More artifacts in storage

Candles stick holders and trunk in choir loft

More candle stickholders in storage

Benito Valdez and his wife Grace Garcia de Valdez were interviewed on April 18, 2011. Benito wanted to do something for the members of the Sagrado Corazón; he said, "[The sociedad] always gives out and never receives anything, so I decided to do something for the members. I presented them with the painting that I had made especially for them. I asked them to hang it wherever they wanted. They said no. They wanted me to hang it wherever I wanted to hang it, so I hung it on the *graditas* of the choir loft." As you walk out of the church, the painting is right on the center of the choir loft. It's a beautiful painting of the Sacred Heart. The stairwell of the painting was intricately made with popsicle sticks.

Gift from Ben Valdez to Sacred Heart Organization

The Sacred Heart Fiesta mass is held every 2nd Friday of June. After the mass celebration a small reception is held, at one time parishioners would walk to what used to be the S.P.M.D.T.U. Hall, now the celebration is held on the church grounds, before he passed away, Adelmo Archuleta spearheaded the event; now his sister Lucille Archuleta de Gonzales and brother-in-law Gilbert continue the tradition—special thanks to them and all the people who helped.

Sacred Heart members before mass: Pablo Romero, Guadalupe Giron, Benito Valdez, and Orlando Ortiz

Sacred Heart members preparing for reception

Lucille Archuleta de Gonazales and helpers for reception

Sacred Heart banner

Going out for procession

Procession on north side of church

Entrance to church after procession

El Cementerio
(El Campo Santo)

There is an old section and a new section of the cemetery. According to folklore, the old section was donated to the community by Cyrus McCormick, but controversy ensues. Some say the new section was purchased by The Archdiocese. Oliver says the property was owned and probably donated to the church by José Gaspar Ortiz and Eliseo Ortiz. As stated earlier, archivist Marina Ochoa, in her research, found a document that states the property was owned and donated by Julian Ortiz, Romolo Luján, José Inez Roybal, José Gaspar Ortiz, and Eliseo Ortiz for the church and the cemetery. In any case, an arroyo ran through part of the cemetery. Ronald Luján (Ronnie) remembers Eloy Herrera taking dirt from a hill, later called *El Pozo*, next to the cemetery, and filling the arroyo with his backhoe.

Our local Boy Scouts took part with their Scout Leaders in the clean-up of the Nambé Cemetery on July 25, 1998. This was done under the direction of Scout Charles Romero, who was working toward the prestigious honor of Eagle Scout. Charles chose this community project, planned it, got help, provided food and followed through until the project was completed.

After the church was plastered in 2001, Father Santillanes said, " now that the church is so beautiful, let's do something about the cemetery." All parishioners who were able to help, got together to clean the cemetery. In an insert to the church bulletin, Father Santillanes and the community of Nambé acknowledge the work done by Toby Martinez, Ernesto, Lydia Herrera de Archuleta, Feliz Garduño, Ben Romero, Oliver Rivera, Barbara Ortiz, Gary Sanchez, Andres Sanchez, Lench Romero, Katherine, Margie Rivera de Roybal, Pete Valdez and his trailer used to haul trash away, Nikki Valdez, Joey Trujillo, Joshua Trujillo, George Luna, and the tractor work—and also— Guillermo, Lorenzo Herrera, Orlando Ortiz, Jerry Garcia, Andres, Jr., Dennis Ortiz, Ronnie Luján, Buddy Montoya, Alfredo Luján, Ernie Luján, Luz Quijada de Lopez, Miquela Lopez de Romero.

The women who prepared food for the *peones* were also acknowledged: Annabelle Lopez de Rivera, Ophelia Romero, Norma Salazar de Trujillo, Virginia Romero de Martinez, and Carrie.

Lorenzo Herrera

Others who have helped clean the cemetery throughout the years are Liza Crespin de Rivera and Gilbert, Carolyn Cordova de Romero and Rick, Rudy Roybal, Jesús Herrera, and Chris Espinoza. We're sure many others helped, but we do not have that information.

George Luna, Joseph Trujillo and son, and Lench

Guillermo Garduño and Jerry Garcia

Oliver Rivera, Pete Valdez, and Ronald Luján

Alfredo Celedón Luján

Margie Rivera de Roybal and Ernie Luján

Ernesto Luján

In addition, Andres Jr. in an interview on May 23, 2012, said he organized about five workers to clean the cemetery. The parish paid them from the cemetery fund. It took them five days to clean the entire cemetery.

People in our community always clean the cemetery at one time or another; some clean their individual family gravesites; others clean all around as much as they can; we all try to keep it presentable, it's almost impossible at times. Most everyone cleans and decorates for Memorial Day.

Recently, the cemetery fence has been replaced by a beautiful wrought iron fence and gate by Chris Espinoza. When asked what inspired him to do this, he said, when his Grandma Eva passed away, he looked around during the burial and saw how bad the old fence was.

In an interview in June 2012, he said that he designed and made the wrought iron gate. Willie (Bill) Ortiz's idea was used for the wrought iron fence. When Chris came with the heavy panels, God helped because Sammy Herrera and Peter Roybal were passing by and asked if he needed any help. He sure did; they helped him unload them.

In addition, many people gave monetary donations from $5.00 to $200.00 for materials. A substantial amount was donated by Willie in memory of his parents José de la Luz and Susanita Luján de Ortiz. When Chris asked Manuel Roybal for a monetary contribution, Manuel said, "I'll do better than that, I will donate materials and labor for the pilastors." Chris expressed much appreciation to Manuel, who along with his crew donated the materials, constructed the pilasters, and plastered them. Gilbert Duran, who had plastered the church gave them the color code so they would match the church. The parish paid for the powder coating. The out-of-pocket cost to Chris was approximately $2,300.00 plus labor.

Chris Espinoza, Adam, Joseph Salazar, and friend

Maria Herrera de Espinoza, Adam Espinoza, and Ronnie Luján

Luben and Lonnie Espinoza

Adam Espinoza, Joseph Salazar, Luben, and Chris Espinoza

Anthony Roybal working on fence

Cemetery Gate

Unplastered pilasters cemetery

Unplastered pilasters

View of church and unplastered pilasters

Unplastered pilasters with Nambé School, barrancas, and Jemez Mountains in background

Plastered cemetery pilasters

Chris also gave credit to all those who helped with the fence, and that includes his mother Maria Herrera de Espinoza, Lonnie, Adam, Alfredo Espinoza, Ronald Luján, Joseph Salazar, Adrian Ortiz, Tony Valdez , and Anthony Roybal.

A cemetery fund exists, through the parish, for anyone who would like to make a donation, as the cemetery continues needing a lot of work.

Memorial for Guadalupe Ortiz de Herrera

Many recent beautiful markers appear in the cemetery now. The ones surrounded by iron gates will last forever. There is one miniature replica of the Sacred Heart Church in honor of the memory of Guadalupe Ortiz de Herrera. Her youngest son, Donald Herrera, had promised his mother that if anything ever happened to her he would do something special for her. He built her this church that sits where she is buried. The miniature church stands four feet tall. It includes tiny stained-glass windows and roof gutters to water the flowers below. It has marble walls, wood floors, a solar-panel system connected to exterior lights that shine on the memorial at night. On Memorial Day for years, Guadalupe and her daughter Lydia Herrera de Archuleta were seen cleaning and decorating the graves of their loved ones. Now we see Lydia with one or another of her siblings decorating her mother's memorial and the memorials of other family members as she and Guadalupe did before.

Vicenta Ortiz de Luján and Eloy Luján memorial

Another memorial is a wall surrounding the graves of Vicenta Ortiz de Luján and Eloy. Their son Ronald (Ronnie) built the wall; it signifies the church, and the two crosses are like the ones on the roof of church. The project history, according to Ronnie, is that he made a concrete ribbon around the two graves. It rained, so he went to check them. He found they were full of water, and that's when he decided a wall to match the church would be more appropriate.

A ledger, started by Benigno and Sofia, and continued by Frances Romero de Luján and her sister, Rumaldita Romero de Romero was shared with Carrie. Because of that list, Ernesto was able to find his grandfather Nestor Lopez's gravesite that had been unknown for many years. Ernesto's family made a wrought iron fence to mark the grave. If it had not been for that ledger, that site may have been lost forever.

A few years back there was a story in *The Santa Fe New Mexican* and in the local news that some headstones were being found in a ditch in a rural community in New Mexico. Upon an investigation, it was discovered that an old uncared-for cemetery was at that location.

If we do not identify the older graves at the Nambé cemetery, the same thing could happen. We, therefore, here publish the ledger so that the descendants of the deceased can more easily find their loved ones. It comes from three different sources (Benigno and Frances Lujan's ledger, Santa Cruz de la Cañada Parish, and Our Lady of Guadalupe Parish), thus the three date formats:

NAMES FROM THE BENIGNO AND FRANCES LEDGER
Date of Death / Name

02/13/1912	José Maria Trujillo	02/08/1918	Emeteria Chaves
04/14/1912	Encarnacion Rodriguez	04/09/1918	Alfonsa Roybal Romero
04/29/1912	Juan Garduño	07/24/1918	Emilia Sandoval
06/13/1912	Clara Rivera	10/18/1918	Francisca Garduño
07/12/1912	Rudolfo Sandoval	10/24/1918	Flavio Ortiz
04/11/1913	Guadalupe Romero	10/26/1918	Albina Salazar
08/---/1913	Antonia Ortiz de Luján	10/26/1918	Virginia Lopez
11/---/1913	Teresa Garduño	10/26/1918	Felicita Lopez
01/23/1914	Aleja Garcia	10/29/1918	Tobias Romero
02/05/1915	Antonio Ortiz Sandoval	10/30/1918	Concesion Garcia
04/19/1914	Antonio Maria Ortiz	11/01/1918	Luciano Garcia
05/20/1914	Benjamin Rivera	11/04/1918	Jacobo Romero
06/25/1914	Gabino Luján	11/04/1918	Concepcion Luján de Sena
03/03/1915	Ignacio Martinez	11/05/1918	Manuelita Roybal de Romero
04/10/1915	Sebero Trujillo	11/06/1918	Josefita Ortiz de Luján
04/24/1915	Francisca Ortiz	11/07/1918	Paulin Gonzales
09/27/1915	Manuel Gonzales	11/07/1918	Ramon Romero
04/02/1916	Francisco Luján	11/10/1918	Nestora Ortiz de Sena
06/21/1916	Enrique Rivera	11/11/1918	Elis Luján de Valdez
08/15/1916	José Remigio Valdes	11/12/1918	Carmelita Ortiz y Garcia
12/19/1916	Eliseo Ortiz	11/15/1918	Senobio Romero
01/26/1917	Alfonsita Luján	11/18/1918	Delfina Catanach
02/15/1917	Rosario Valdez	11/26/1918	Lucia Ortiz
03/10/1917	Josefa Luján	12/24/1918	Eluteria Sena
08/30/1917	José R. Rivera	11/22/1919	Atoche Romero
10/23/1917	Camila Sanchez	12/27/1919	José Gabriel Ortiz
10/31/1917	Elisaria Romero Herrera	05/30/1920	Manuelita Ortiz de Herrera
12/10/1917	Juan José Ortiz	09/28/1920	Antonio Archuleta
12/30/1917	Guadalupe Rivera Sandoval	12/19/1920	Natividad Sandoval

03/08/1921	Patrocinia Sandoval de Romero	10/10/1927	Meliton Ortiz
		10/28/1927	Angelita Romero Rivera
03/11/1921	Alejo Garduño	11/21/1927	Josefita Luján
03/30/1921	Antonia Ortiz	12/11/1927	Pablo Valdez
05/29/1921	Elvira Sandoval	02/26/1928	Paz Roibal
07/11/1921	Narciso Quintana	05/31/1928	Maria Encarnacion Gonzales
06/28/1922	José L. Sandoval	07/08/1928	Ignacio Garcia
03/14/1923	Maria Ines Luján	07/09/1928	Abelina Ortiz Luján
01/03/1924	Pedro Ignacio Ortiz	10/22/1928	Simon Romero
02/08/1924	Sofia Martinez	06/18/1928	Miguel Herreera
08/11/1924	Pacomio Ortiz	11/16/1928	Elidiora Sandoval Garduño
08/29/1924	Libradita Trujillo	11/16/1928	Elidiora Sandoval Garduño
12/12/1924	Cosme Garcia	12/17/1928	Esquipula Valdez Ortiz
01/31/1925	Juan O. Romero	--------------	Juan B. Romero
04/06/1925	Edwardo Quintana	O5/30/1929	Estefanita Herrera Luján
06/14/1925	Emiliana Lopez	07/26/1929	Pedro Garduño
03/15/1926	Gregorita Luján	07/27/1929	Casimiro Herrera
06/10/1926	José Leon Garduño	09/14/1929	Julio Garduño
06/26/1926	Reyecita Quintana	01/26/1930	Ramona Romero Martinez
09/29/1926	Nestor Lopez	04/15/1930	Macimiona Romero
10/20/1926	Eustaquo Herrera (is buried in same fence with Reyecita Quintana and Julian Ortiz)	06/29/1930	Eufelio Sandoval
		09/01/1930	Antonio Sena
		12/04/1930	Adelina Romero
11/18/1926	Julian Ortiz (is buried in same fence next to Reyecita Quintana)	12/19/1930	Guadalupe Ortiz
		02/13/1931	Ana Maria Valdez Garduño
		03/01/1931	Romolo Luján
11/27/1926	Federico Romero	03/18/1931	Nolasco Romero
12/31/1926	Tiburcia Maestas	08/04/1931	Jacinto Garduño
01/07/1927	Teresa Garcia	09/05/1931	Manuel Herrera
03/17/1927	Benseslado Garduño	09/08/1931	Maximiliano Romero
07/17/1927	Gumesindo Vigil	10/07/1931	Cesario H Ortiz
09/06/1927	Tomacita Romero Rivera	11/06/1931	Amalia Ruybal Gomez
09/28/1927	Juanita Chacon Romero	03/13/1932	Sara Ortiz
09/30/1927	Paublita Quintana Ortiz	03/18/1932	Cecilio Luján

05/17/1932	Nasario Valdez	12/02/1937	Bernardo Romero (father
06/22/1932	Francisquita Montoya		Vidal Romero)
	Romero	01/15/1938	Antonio Sena (father Severo
09/19/1932	Julio Roybal		Sena)
10/07/1932	José Inez Roybal	04/12/1938	Trinidad G. Romero (wife to
10/14/1932	Eliseo Luján		Patrocinio Romero)
02/10/1933	Julianita Gonzales	09/19/1938	Antonio Ortiz y Rivera
02/24/1933	Nabor Gomez		(before Benigno)
03/25/1933	Bisenta Ortiz	02/11/1939	Rosina O. Garcia
04/03/1933	Crestino Vigil	02/22/1939	Catalino Luján
09/23/1933	Jesucito Lopez	04/03/1939	Ramon Garcia
09/16/1933	Manuelita Ortiz	09/01/1939	Rafael Ortiz y Romero
10/08/1933	Desiderio Ortiz	-------/1940	Tomacita S. Archuleta
12/14/1933	Belarmino Romero	06/08/1940	Sostenes Ortiz
03/06/1934	Sebero Ortiz	11/13/1940	Ramon Valdez
03/23/1934	Ramon Luján	03/14/1941	Juana Valdez
03/26/1934	Elberia Roybal (este cuerpo	03/31/1941	Beatrice Sandoval
	esta internado al lado de	04/04/1941	Reymundo Ortiz
	JQR)	-------/1941	Francisco Romero (enfrente
04/25/1934	Matilde Sena		de Beatrice Sandoval)
08/04/1934	Antonia Valdez	07/20/1941	Severo Sena
08/04/1934	Crucitas Alire	08/26/1941	Regina Ortiz
03/10/1935	Senaida Luján	-------/1941	Eduvijen Valdez (wife to
03/17/1935	Grabiel Valdez		Pablo Valdez)
03/21/1935	Benigno Romero (sepultado	11/29/1941	José Crescencio Sandoval
	enfrente de Belarmino	12/27/1941	Emeterio Rivera
	Romero)	03/19/1942	Todosio Ortiz
05/30/1935	Ramon Garcia Valdez	04/11/1942	Luis Valdez
10/10/1935	Federico Ortiz	06/26/1942	Antonia Quintana
04/03/1936	Niño de Pablo Martinez, Jr.	07/13/1942	Miguel Valdez
02/28/1937	Beronis Martinez Lopez	08/19/1942	Epimenia S. Ortiz
03/30/1937	Aurelio Roybal	09/06/1942	Pablina Garcia
10/21/1937	Lupita Sena	11/01/1942	Fermin Garcia
10/22/1937	Bernabe Garcia	01/25/1943	Agapito Herrera

-------/1943	Nicolas Sena
07/17/1943	Antonio Onofre Gomez
05/25/1943	Alberto Ortiz
01/27/1943	Epifanio Valdez
04/11/1943	Mersedes Garduño
06/20/1944	Florencia Salazar (or Florencio)
07/23/1944	Manuel Lopez
10/31/1944	Cleto Montoya
11/20/1944	Virginia Romero

INFANTS BURIED IN THE SACRED HEART CEMETERY

(NIÑOS SEPULTADOS EN EL CEMETERIO DEL SAGRADO CORAZON DE JESUS EN NAMBÉ, NUEVO MEXICO)

06/08/1913	Niño de Eliseo Luján	01/02/1922	Niña Epifania Ortiz
08/12/1913	Niño de Eliseo Roybal	01/11/1922	Niña Audelia Ortiz
02/26/------	Niño de José A. Sandoval	03/27/1922	Niña de Luis Ortiz
03/03/1916	Paulito Romero	04/02/1922	Niña de Leopoldo Ortiz
03/03/1916	Francisquita Luján, Niña de Celedon Luján	05/21/1922	Niña de Ambrocio Trujillo
		07/30/1922	Niña Rosina Luján
05/20/1916	Refujito Romero	08/---/1922	Niño Juan Martinez
06/24/1916	Niño Felipe Gonzales	09/13/1922	Niño José Luis D. Luján
--------------	Niño de Mercedes Vigil	10/22/1922	Bitoriana Garduño Niño
12/27/1917	Niño de José C. Sandoval		Guilfredo Valdez
05/15/1918	Niño de Elias Archuleta	12/03/1922	Niño Rosinaldo Ortiz
07/27/1918	Niña Adelicia Luján	01/21/1923	Niño de Enrique Romero
01/20/1918	Rosarito Luján Niña de Celedon Luján	02/01/1923	Niño Esequiel Luján Niño de Celedon Luján
01/20/1919	Esequiel Luján (Niño de Celedon Luján	02/04/1923	Niño de Gregorio Lopez
		02/14/1923	Niña Rebecca Luján
08/08/1920	Niña Ursulita Martinez	03/09/1923	Niña Maria Lydia Romero
12/29/1920	Niña de Ramon Roybal	09/17/1923	Niña Abenilda Montoya
02/10/1921	Niño de Felix Romero	09/30/1923	Magalena Angelina Montoya
05/10/1921	Niño de José A. Romero	10/07/1923	Natividad Montoya
05/22/1921	Niño de José Valdez	10/18/1923	Niña Bicentita Martinez
06/03/1921	Niño de Canuto Romero	12/14/1923	Niña Erlinda Romero
07/06/1921	Niño de Esequiel Ortiz	12/27/1923	Manuelita Ortiz
07/13/1921	Niño de José R. Valdez	12/31/1923	Niño Benancio Ortiz
09/05/1921	Niño de Atanacio Romero	03/11/1924	Merejildo Martinez
10/---/1921	Niño de Eliseo Luján	07/29/1924	Tomacito Luján
12/27/1921	Niña Eufelia Ortiz	09/12/1924	Bictoriano Ortiz
12/29/1921	Niña Josefita Valdez	09/29/1924	Niño de Juan B. Gomez

12/05/1924	Maximineo Valdez	08/29/1929	Niño de Fermin Garcia
01/30/1925	Niño Gilbert Salazar	09/01/1929	Niño de Onofre Ortiz
03/30/1925	Niño de Juan Luján	09/13/1929	Niño de José C. Romero
06/03/1925	Niño de Ricardo Saiz	09/21/1929	Niño de Adelaido Ribera
06/24/1925	Niño de Eliseo Luján	10/06/1929	Niño de Melecio Gallegos
08/24/1925	Niño de Florentino Ortiz	10/09/1929	Niño de Gregorio Martinez
09/24/1925	Niño de José E. Romero	10/12/1929	Niño de Gregorio Martinez
09/27/1925	Niño de Audelia Valdez		(must've been twins)
04/17/1926	Niña Josefina Valdez	03/09/1930	Niña Maria Salome Romero
10/03/1926	Niño de Juan B. Gomez	03/11/1930	Niño de Lorenzo Luján
01/08/1927	Niño de Doroteo Ortiz	04/16/1930	Benigno Archuleta
01/24/1927	Niña Audelia Roibal	06/09/1930	Elionora Martinez
04/14/1927	Niña de Tomas Catanach	08/09/1930	José R. Isauro Valdez
05/07/1927	Niño de Seferino Luján	09/27/1930	Niño de José Eugenio Romero
07/31/1927	Niño Juan Luis Quintana	03/18/1931	Niña Gabrielita Valdez
08/04/1927	Niño de Canuto Romero	04/03/1931	Niño de Adolfo Madrid
08/12/1927	Niña Libradita Ortiz	04/08/1931	Niña de José de La Cruz
08/12/1927	Niño Juan O. Romero		Romero
08/16/1927	Niño de Pedro S. Luján	05/12/1931	Niño de Miguel Herrera
09/11/1927	Niña Eulalia Rivera	06/02/1931	Niño de Miguel Herrera
10/17/1927	Niño Gilberto Herrera		(must've been twins)
10/21/1927	Niña Elaisa Sena	06/02/1931	Niño de Daniel Rael
12/27/1927	Niño de Abenicio Trujillo	08/09/1931	Niño de Herminio Sandoval
01/02/1928	Niño de José E. Romero	08/20/1931	Niña de Enrique Ortiz
01/20/1928	Niña de Bernardino Herrera	09/28/1931	Niño de Esperanza Herrera
04/02/1928	Niño de Pablo Herrera	10/29/1931	Niño de Celestino Gomez
08/19/1928	Niño de Ricardo Saiz	11/07/1931	Niño de Inez Valdez, Gilberto
09/12/1928	Niño Onofre Ortiz	03/02/1932	Josefina Herrera
12/14/1928	Niña de Doroteo Ortiz	03/07/1932	Niño de Martiniano Romero
12/16/1928	Maria Juana	03/12/1932	Niña de Eugenio Garduño
01/29/1929	Niño de Celina Luján	05/02/1932	Niño de Damian Ortiz
02/09/1929	Niña de Juan Rivera	06/14/1932	Niña Masedona
08/18/1929	Niño-------Luján	10/14/1932	Leopoldo Ortiz
08/20/1929	Niño de Seferino Luján	10/30/1932	Niño de Secundino Romero

11/09/1932	Niño de Fermin Garcia	06/14/1937	Niño de Juan Luján
02/05/1933	Niño de Antonio Garcia	07/18/1937	Niño de Luis Valdez
08/04/1933	Niña de Ricardo Herrera	07/26/1937	Niño de Manuel A. Trujillo
01/23/1934	Niño de Luis Valdez	-------/1937	Niño de Eliseo Gomez
03/09/1934	Niño Andres Florentino Ortiz	12/24/1937	Niño de Frank Garcia
03/21/1934	Dolesito Ortiz	04/09/1938	Niño de Patrocinio Romero
06/13/1934	Niña Maria Isabel Josefita Romero	09/10/1938	Niño de Ricardo Herrera
		10/16/1938	Niño de Federico Garduño
08/30/1934	Niño de Leopoldo Ortiz	12/02/1938	Niño de Praxedes Lopez
10/18/1934	Niño de Antonio Garduño	01/---/1939	Niña de Antonio Garduño
11/04/1934	Niño de Willie Quintana	-------/1939	Niña de Cruz Romero
02/01/1935	Niño de Luiz Valdez	-------/1939	Niña de Pedro Lopez
02/19/1935	Niño Romolo Luján de Celedon Luján	-------/1939	Niño de Juan Luján y Ortiz
		07/---/1939	Niña de Teresina Luján
03/08/1935	Niño de Federico Quintana	08/11/1939	Niño de Eliud Ortiz
05/23/1935	Niño de Leopoldo Ortiz	-------/1939	Niño de Dominico Luján
05/26/1935	Maria Juana, Niña de Augustin Romero	07/---/1940	Niña de Juan Ortiz
		08/28/1940	Niño de José Trujillo
09/15/1935	Niño de Cruz Romero	08/28/1940	Niño de Eliseo Gomez
11/22/1935	Niña de Ramon Vigil, Feliz Graciola	08/28/1940	Niño de Carmen Romero
		08/28/1940	Niño de Federico Quintana
12/11/1935	Niño de Willie Quintana	08/28/1940	Niño de Eliud Ortiz (sepultado enfrente de Ruperto Ortiz)
09/17/1936	Niña de Ramon Vigil Berlin Yolanda		
		08/07/1941	Niño de Leopoldo Ortiz
09/19/1936	Niña de Adenois Luján	08/22/1941	Niña de Eloy Herrera
10/10/1936	Niño de Modesto Romero	02/01/1942	Niña Juanita Madril
11/---/1936	Niño de Willie Quintana	03/20/1942	Niña Maria Lilian (?)
11/18/1936	Niña de Ricardo Herrera	03/30/1942	Niño de Felipe Valdez
11/20/1936	Niño de Ramon Romero		
12/12/1936	Niña de Estevan Archuleta		
01/12/1937-	Niño de Juan Gomez Wilfredo Genaro		
06/03/1937	Niña de Martiniano Romero, Sofia Romero		

NAMES FROM THE *SANTA CRUZ DE LA CAÑADA* LEDGER
Date of Death / Name / Age at Time of Death

Date	Name	Age	Date	Name	Age
03/25/1945	Antonio Luján	90	03/19/1950	José Gilberto Ortiz	23
04/29/1945	Patricia Martinez	52	03/26/1950	Rosario Ortiz	83
09/18/1945	José Anselmo Martinez	19	10/04/1950	Antonio Romero	78
12/17/1945	José Vicente Romero	65	01/02/1951	Oliver Narvaiz	26
01/21/1946	Hilario Branch	77	01/27/1951	Josefita Ortiz	93
01/23/1946	José Angel Gomez	66	07/05/1951	Juan R. Luján	63
02/06/1946	Ramos Luján	32	03/16/1952	Juan B. Ribera	
11/30/1946	Martina Martinez	70	07/01/1952	Adrian Herrera	44
01/20/1947	Tranquilino Vigil	50	10/14/1952	José O. Ortiz	25
01/29/1947	Victoriana Garcia	48	01/18/1953	Avelina O. Sena	88
02/22/1948	Josefita Ortiz	78	04/24/1953	Camilo Garcia	
03/01/1948	Felipe Quintana	43	07/30/1953	Maximiana L. Ortiz	87
05/13/1948	Antonio Garduño	45	11/19/1953	Maria Paz Romero	74
05/22/1948	Enrique Romero	45	11/22/1953	Vitalia Rivera	72
08/16/1948	Wilfredo Sandoval	17	03/05/1954	Elizeo Luján	66
08/18/1948	Rosana Ortiz	48	01/10/1954	Fermin Luján	79
09/05/1948	Juana M. Ortiz	75	03/07/1955	Pedro Rivera	91
09/27/1948	Seferino Valdez	42	05/20/1955	Donaciano Ortiz	82
11/13/1948	Ambrosia V. Garduño	98	11/03/1955	Leroy Salazar	17. mo.
12/08/1948	Simplicia E. Luján	58	04/11/1956	Nicanora R. Sandoval	79
01/30/1949	Gregorita Luján	88	05/20/1956	Luisita Rivera	85
03/03/1949	Crescenciana Valdez	39	05/24/1956	Sofia V. Garcia	63
03/23/1949	José Gregorio Lopez	56	12/19/1956	Darlene Luján	5 yrs.o
06/02/1949	Maria Eduvigen Valdez	79	02/15/1957	Matias Romero	95
07/10/1949	Maria Lina Roybal	75	06/19/1957	Basilia Ortiz	94
09/15/1949	Ramona Lopez de Romero	68	09/12/1957	Petronila Rivera	
12/21/1949	Juan Ortiz	55	03/10/1958	Elias Archuleta	64
12/25/1949	Agapito Herrera	36	04/09/1958	Abel Ortiz	88
02/07/1950	Eugenio Garduño	61	05/18/1958	Maximiliano Martinez	85
03/15/1950	Ramon Rivera	76	08/05/1958	Rafael Ortiz	80

NAMES FROM OUR LADY OF GUADALUPE LEDGER
Date of Death / Name / Age at Time of Death

Date	Name	Age	Date	Name	Age
04/09/1959	Seferina Ortiz	84	10/16/1965	Federico Salazar	78
04/11/1959	Henry Ortiz	53	02/01/1966	Nestor Sandoval	73
05/04/1959	Roberta Ann Gonzales	7 mo.	02/20/1966	Ignacita Luján	72
01/11/1960	Encarnacion Sandoval	90	04/01/1966	Valentin R. Valdez	68
01/13/1960	José Inez Valdez	67	05/02/1966	Merced Sandoval	83
03/08/1960	Abenicio Trujillo	63	07/05/1966	Antonia Terrazas	63
03/10/1960	Maria Eduvigen Romero	37	09/08/1966	Jeronimo Valdez	49
06/10/1960	Tomas Martinez	51	09/11/1966	Luis Ortiz	78
08/08/1960	Eliu Ortiz	54	09/27/1967	Manuelita Herrera	84
02/08/1961	Frank Valdez	72	11/23/1967	Adolfo Madrid	62
05/28/1961	Aguinaldo Gomez	39	12/27/1967	Teresina Romero	52
06/27/1961	Martiniano Romero	57	01/22/1968	Petronila Luján	70
02/24/1962	Vidal Romero	82	02/08/1968	Rudolfo Herreera	51
03/04/1962	Pedro Luján	69	05/09/1968	Tomas Gurduno	78
03/12/1962	Pablo Romero	79	06/30/1968	Henrietta Romero	74
05/06/1962	Luciana Archuleta	72	09/21/1968	Eva R. Montoya	62
03/19/1963	Juanita Baca	74	11/01/1968	Enriqueta H. Rodriguez	63
06/09/1963	Ramona Vigil	78	11/28/1968	Dominico Luján	71
10/16/1963	Esther Herrera	76	12/01/1968	Librado Valdez	92
03/21/1964	Aurelia Garduño	68	12/07/1968	Jacobo Garduño	99
03/29/1964	Esquipula Valdez	62	12/28/1968	Feliberto Ortiz	80
04/11/1964	José Longino Quintana	81	06/25/1969	Juan B. Gomez	81
05/10/1964	Francisquita Roybal	69	11/03/1969	Joaquin Garduño	84
05/14/1964	José A. Sandoval	88	02/28/1970	Bersabella Garcia	90
05/28/1964	Eliza Lopez	75	03/11/1970	Leopoldo Ortiz	65
01/23/1965	Rojelio Valdez	54	01/29/1971	Julianita Ortiz	88
04/10/1965	Amada H. Garcia	81	03/05/1971	Edwardo Ortiz	77
07/19/1965	José Dolores Sandoval	58	06/14/1971	José Sandoval	45
			08/24/1971	Aguinaldo Roybal	71

10/30/1971	Rudy Quintana	39	08/24/1977	Altagracia Romero	72
11/21/1971	Stephen Daniel Martinez	6 weeks.	12/02/1977	Margarita Garcia	79
12/15/1971	Petra Romero	90	12/25/1977	Eulogia Valdez	72
12/23/1971	Teresa Valdez	18	01/05/1978	Seferino Luján	78
01/15/1972	Eliseo Gomez	80	03/16/1978	Cecelia R. Baca	72
01/22/1972	Juanita Valdez	73	05/03/1978	José L. Ortiz	70
02/02/1972	Catalino Ortiz	66	10/25/1978	Andreita Sandoval	85
03/18/1972	Edwardo Rodriguez	69	11/20/1978	Lino B. Ortiz	42
04/13/1972	Rosendo Romero	73	11/20/1978	Vicente Ortiz	34
04/26/1972	Ramos Vigil	23	01/20/1979	Pablita Sandoval	94
09/08/1972	Juan A. Gomez	74	06/03/1979	Abel L. Montoya	80
01/19/1973	Flora Gomez	73	08/28/1979	Rudy Gomez	39
01/07/1973	Maria Gomez	67	09/07/1979	Edith Lopez	33
07/16/1973	Hilario Valdez	51	10/05/1979	Teresina Sandoval	74
08/13/1973	Viola Valdez	48	O2/13/1980	Telesfor Romero	85
09/01/1973	José Guadalupe Lazaro Herrera	38	05/26/1980	Eligio Griego	38
09/26/1973	David Herrera	95	08/14/1980	Ignacita Valdez	No age
10/21/1973	Estevan Sandoval	19	10/08/1980	Enriques Romero	85
12/16/1973	Monico Benavidez	No age	12/29/1980	Cleotilde Ortiz	85
02/05/1974	Antionette Elaine Salazar	Infant	02/06/1981	Manuel Ortiz	68
04/25/1974	Maclovio Lopez	50	08/20/1981	Celestina Romero	90
05/05/1974	Estevan Archuleta	78	10/28/1981	Maria Roybal	80
05/21/1974	Beatriz Herrera	90	12/10/1981	Procopio Romero	63
06/21/1974	Vianes Valdez	43	01/20/1982	Bernardo Baca	87
03/07/1975	Frutoso Herreera	95	02/05/1982	Rosendo Sandoval	86
04/08/1975	Amadeo Ortiz	62	02/12/1982	Candelaria Luján	80
05/31/1975	Gary Gomez	22	03/21/1982	Rufina Salazar	90
09/19/1975	Felipe Valdez	71	10/10/1982	Ramon Montoya	78
09/22/1975	Bernardita Luján	73	12/23/1982	Olympia Mondragon	57
09/25/1975	Frank Romero	56	02/05/1983	Marcelina Romero	89
09/29/1975	Juan Romero	66	06/18/1983	Salomon Trujillo	51
03/24/1976	Emiliano Lopez	91	11/05/1983	José Felix Romero	96
04/01/1976	Rosina Leyba	50	11/29/1983	Celedonio Luján	97
01/07/1977	Otilia L. Lopez	60	03/03/1984	José A. Rivera	77

05/09/1984	Nestora L. Luján	88	06/04/1993	Amabe Garduño	80
10/21/1984	Antonia Herrera	69	07/18/1993	Grisiela Madrid	66
11/26/1984	Amabel Lopez	62	10/14/1993	Guillermo (Willie) Romero	54
01/28/1985	José R. Valdez	90	02/19/1994	Teofilo L. Lopez	76
12/19/1984	David Gomez	22	03/23/1994	Pacifica Garcia	88
03/01/1985	Elena Ortiz	74	06/22/1994	Eluteria Ortiz	79
12/06/1985	Adelia G. Benavidez	86	01/19/1995	Bernardita (Bernie) Rivera	79
01/28/1986	José Elvirio Ortiz	70	08/31/1995	Juanita Rivera Romero	85
10/22/1986	Luis Romero	86	09/07/1995	Esperanza Herrera	91
06/20/1987	Eloy Herrera	74	10/12/1995	Sabina G. Herrera	82
09/15/1987	José Manuel Ortiz	85	12/10/1995	Vicenta Teresa Luján	71
09/28/1987	Michael A. Ortiz	25	12/15/1995	Andreita Gomez	86
10/05/1987	Delfina Madrid	78	01/05/1996	Julian Manuel Gomez, Jr.	37
10/31/1987	Herminio Sandoval	82	02/28/1996	Sostenes Rivera	88
12/12/1987	Sarah Luján	7 mo.	05/11/1996	José Belarmino Sandoval	57
03/06/1988	Fidencio Baca	99	06/11/1996	Ramon A. Ortiz	59
04/07/1988	Senaida Romero	81	12/24/1996	Catalino Jimenez	66
05/05/1988	Sarita Ortiz	79	01/15/1997	Maria Reyecita Longacre	62
10/12/1988	Regina Romero	88	01/28/1997	Praxedes Lopez	82
08/25/1989	José Isadias Ortiz	60	06/19/1997	Luis Ramon Luján	23
12/08/1989	Gavino Rivera	85	08/09/1997	Ronald Lee Megariz	33
05/15/1990	Rita Salazar	88	08/28/1997	Eva O. Valdez	91
08/26/1990	Helen G. Luján	69	05/21/1998	Augustine Romero	95
12/01/1990	Paul Joseph Mondragon	28	07/20/1998	Samuel Ortiz	
12/19/1990	Paublita Ortiz	92		(parents Abel/Teodora)	78
12/26/1990	Esquipula Salazar	94	08/14/1998	Stephen R. Herrera	48
01/04/1991	Lucy Salazar	57	12/05/1998	John Patrick Gonzales	44
03/06/1991	Rebecca S. Romero	93	12/29/1998	Ramon Herrera	77
07/30/1991	Sofia Romero	90	01/25/1999	Victoriana Ortiz	87
02/05/1992	José Benancio Valdez	64	09/09/1999	Fidelia Rivera	93
04/26/1992	Manuel Tony Archuleta	67	10/11/1999	Solomon Luna	85
10/28/1992`	Angelo Frank Romero	50	01/03/2000	Juan J. Luján	87
04/13/1993	Ignacio Sandoval	74	01/24/2000	Rueben Rivera	96
05/22/1993	José Leroy Montoya	58	03/23/2000	Freddie Salazar	69

Date	Name	Age
04/26/2000	José Maria Herrera	53
08/22/2000	Vidal Santos Romero	22
01/31/2001	Patrocinio Romero	88
05/19/2001	Josefa Ortiz	88
05/27/2001	Danny Paul Roybal	33
07/18/2001	Luis V. Luján	65
02/04/2002	Gilbert Salazar	71
02/27/2002	Celia V. Herrera	80
05/04/2002	Juan P. Romero	76
06/24/2002	Emily Gomez	71
09/14/2002	Eloy Luján, Sr.	85
10/12/2002	José Serafin Trujillo	89
01/26/2002	Hilario (Larry) Gomez	73
03/22/2003	Pablo Gomez	71
05/28/2003	José Toby Martinez	72
06/13/2003	Esther T. Mendiola	77
07/07/2003	Kenneth Ortiz	38
03/30/2004	Carmel Romero	95
08/17/2004	Anselmo V. Valdez	95
08/25/2004	Rudy Rivera	52
05/13/2005	Vanessa Kateri Herrera	18
06/05/2005	Onofre M. Garcia (buried with her father Nabor Maestas)	91
08/25/2005	Ida Romero Trujillo	88
09/15/2005	Ronald Gould	17
09/28/2005	Elizardo Ortiz	89
10/24/2005	Maria Amada Romero	86
10/29/2005	Alfredo Quintana	50
11/23/2005	Robert D. Trujillo, Jr.	20
01/20/2006	Vernon Brown	40
01/21/2006	Abelino Casados	85
03/07/2006	Eliza Montoya Rivera	96
04/10/2006	Mary Zamora	75
04/17/2006	Inez V. Encinias Garcia	74
07/12/2006	Susanita Luján Ortiz	95
12/27/2006	Adelicia Ortiz Luna	90
01/26/2007	Frances Maestas Montoya	98
02/28/2007	Margaret Gomez Morrison	61
04/15/2007	Frances Marie Vigil	44
06/18/2007	Levi Baca	41
07/20/2007	Angel L. Romero (cremated and buried with his father)	30
07/23/2007	Aurelia Sena Romero Martinez	97
07/21/2007	Gary H. Duran	23
08/15/2007	Romolo Romero	67
10/15/2007	Rebecca Ortiz Archuleta	101
12/08/2007	Audrey Martinez (cremated and buried with her father)	33
12/06/2007	Manuelita Herrera	23
01/27/2008	Cornelio Herrera, Sr.	96
02/14/2008	Norman J. Gomez	46
02/16/2008	Casilda Ortiz	89
03/02/2008	Lucinda Rivera Sandoval	99
04/14/2008	Guadalupe O. Herrera	85
05/18/2008	Vincent Charles Lopez	43
07/05/2008	Stephanie Louise Herrera	32
09/16/2008	Juanita Romero (aunt to Alberto Baca)	96
10/07/2008	Gary Paul Romero	45
12/21/2008	José Ramon Romero	98
05/09/2009	Stella B. Quintana	85
07/20/2009	Gilbert M. Romero	75
01/05/2010	Raymond J. Gomez	35
04/11/2010	Bernardino J. Valdez	41
06/04/2010	Elvira Valdez	97
01/26/2011	Leland James Rogelio Valdez	3 years.
02/17/2011	Alberto (Epimenio) Baca	86
02/20/2011	Christina Rivera Hyde	65

03/15/2011	Lucas José Augustine Duran	81
05/13/2011	Abel A. Gomez (Tony)	75
05/12/2011	Mary M. Romero	89
06/29/2011	Esquipula N. Valdez	74
10/27/2011	Anthony John Valdez	27
11/03/2011	Juan Elizario Montoya	81
11/19/2011	Loretta Mae Ortiz	66
11/20/2011	Michael Joseph Roybal	61
12/29/2011	Benito J. Valdez	77
01/18/2012	Eulalio Matthew Molina	19
04/28/2012	Frances R. Romero	101
05/13/2012	Richard C. Sandoval (buried with his father José D. Sandoval	71
06/08/2012	George Fernandez	80
10/26/2012	Ponciano (Ponce) Luján	79
12/18/2012	Ben Luján, Speaker of the House	77

Acknowledgements

For the incredible, painstaking hours, days, months, and years of research and interviews for this book—to all who have helped—God bless.

Matthew O'Keefe for the photography

Arturo A. Romero for contributing his photograph of the Corpus Christi altar

Anthony Luján for his depiction of the old church that burned down, based on Richard Sandoval's painting

Tom Farrell, teacher at Pojoaque Middle School, for scanning the photos in the First Edition, 1997

The Pojoaque Valley Schools

Dionicio Ortiz and Ortiz Printing for the original printing back in 1947

Ralph Ortiz and Ortiz Printing for the remarkable contribution of time, printing, and materials, 1997

Fred, Anne, Rick, and all the Ortiz family for the Ortiz Designed medallions and contributions

Chendo Roybal for the use of his scaffolds

Robert Romero's Hauling

Juan Borrego Trucking

Herrera Brothers' Sand and Gravel

I. M. Roybal

Norma Salazar de Trujillo and Arsenio

José Ramon Romero for the use of his tractor

Tina Bueno de Herrera and Osmundo

Armando Luján

Fred Salazar

Guillermo Garduño

Luben Espinoza

Michael Luján, Jr.

John Dominguez and Dominguez Carpet

Manuel Martinez

Marcos Trujillo

The Sagrado Corazon Cofradía

Lorenzo Herrera

Carolina M. Romero de Luján and Ernesto

Gilbert Ortiz

Sophie Romero de Vigil and Longino

Claudine Ortiz de Armenta and Larry

Lucille Archuleta de Gonzales and Gilbert

Luz Quesada de Lopez and Leonard

Monica Martinez de Ortiz and Gabriel

Nestora Roybal de Garduño and Gilbert

Annabelle Lopez de Rivera and Oliver

Toni Tapia de Romero

Leisha Armijo

Angie Serna de Martinez

Meade and Robin Martin

Benigno Romero, Frances Romero de Luján, and Rumaldita Romero de Romero

Staff at Santa Cruz de La Cañada

Staff at Our Lady Guadalupe Parish

Staff at The New Mexico Archives

Marina Ochoa from the Archdiocese Archives

Staff at The New Mexico History Library

The Santa Fe New Mexican

Longino Vigil, Ernesto Luján, Osmundo Herrera, David Herrera, and Manuel Martinez for work on Bulto en Nicho

Cleo Romero for tin frame

Jorge Trujillo for tin frame

Father Flavio Santillanes

Helen Romero de Luján for sharing the photograph of the Otowi Bridge

Virginia Romero de Martinez for sharing her photographs of Domitilia and Pasqual

Ronald Luján for sharing his photographs of the cemetery

Oliver Rivera for the tremendous amount of information and sharing of his map of the cemetery

Frank Lopez, Jr. for sharing his extensive knowledge and expertise

Marcella Sandoval for her advice regarding the publishing of the book

Richard Sandoval's painting of the original church

Reverend Monsignor Jerome Martinez y Alire for his most excellent proofreading

Cara Esquibel, teacher at Monte de Sol Charter School, for editing the Spanish

Kiana Maldonado for helping with the Spanish editing

Amadeo Hughes Sanchez for helping with photo editing

Contributions for this book were also made by:

Andres Garcia, Sr., Andres Garcia, Jr., Domitilia Garduño de Chavez and Pasqual, Teresita Romero de Sandoval, Luben Espinoza, Hilario Gomez, José Gonzales, Lorenzo Herrera, Ismael Ernesto Luján, Medardo Luján, Fern Montoya de Giron, Elizardo Ortiz, Elvirio Ortiz, Gilbert Ortiz, Fedelina Garduño de Ortiz, Mary Ortiz de Romero and Arturo A., Medardo Ortiz, Angela Rivera de Lopez, José Ramon Romero, Ramoncito "Ray" Romero, Meliton Roybal, Longino Vigil, Grace Garcia de Valdez and Benito, Chris Espinoza, Emily Ortiz de Luján, Ronald Luján, José Herminio Garcia, Donaldo Roybal, Pablo Romero, Frances Romero de Luján, Deacon John Archuleta,

Deacon Reuben Roybal, Robert Skaggs, Juanita Sandoval de Misere, Lydia Herrera de Archuleta, Lawrence Herrera, Ophelia Romero, José Ben Gonzales, Willie (Bill) Ortiz, Ronnie Duran, Gilbert Duran, and Robert Duran. Oliver Rivera, and Pedro Nolasco "Pete N." Romero

Conclusion

It has been a pleasure spending quality time with my Mother, Carrie, working on this Church History project: *Counting Our Blessings*. Over the years I have found her to be a true archivist and editor. She is somewhat a perfectionist … one who finds every misplaced tab or space or comma or misspelling (frustrating!) … one who has to get all the facts straight. She worked very hard to get the history straight and to solicit contributions to the story. Yet … even with her constant attention to the project and seemingly endless revisions, there may be errors or omissions that are not intended. We leave it to the readers to revise this history when the time comes.

Some readers may find it troubling that the sections in the book are neither arranged chronologically, nor are they clustered thematically. One reason for this is that many of the photos in the book were labeled and inserted as we went along. Plus— it is written in the oral tradition of northern New Mexico—told as it came to mind. To re-arrange the book chronologically or thematically would mean re-numbering the photos and re-inserting them. It may also appear that there are redundancies between "Acknowledgements" and "Contributions to the Story," but, in fact, many parishioners contributed in more ways than one. It was our decision to leave as is. It is now time to publish.

It was great meeting mom in her office/computer room many times because those special moments were usually accompanied by *un caldito* or some other *sabroso* dish like *frijolitos con chile, carne adobada* or a bologna sandwich with mustard and green *chile* on a toasted *tortillita*. It was great meeting her and her chauffeur—Ernesto

(Dad)—driving Miss Carrie—at restaurants or coffee shops, where we'd spread our notes and computer and get to work. I did much of the writing and the documentation of her findings. She was on task for *so* many hours, days, weeks, months, years … making sure everything was right by doing the research and conducting interviews. Watching her work through this project has made me very proud of mom, as if I weren't already.

I have but one thing left to say to her: "*…el día que tú naciste, nacieron todas las flores…*" ("*Las Mañanitas*").

Sources

"2,500 Attend Blessing of New Nambe Church by Archbishop." *Santa Fe New Mexican* [Santa Fe, New Mexico] 31 March 1947, n. pag. Print.

"50 Year Anniversary." *Iglesia del Sagarado Corazón de Jesús, Nambe.* 1997.

Archbishop of Santa Fe. "Letter to Reverend Gene Salvador, S.F." 3 June 1946.

Archbishop of Santa Fe. "Letter to Most Reverend William D. O'Brian, D.D." 21 October 1946.

"Bulletin." *Nuestra Señora de Guadalupe del Valle de Pojoaque.* April 15, 2012.

"Bulletin." *Nuestra Señora de Guadalupe del Valle de Pojoaque.* August 2, 1998.

"Bulletin." *Nuestra Señora de Guadalupe del Valle de Pojoaque.* June 17, 2012.

Byrne, Most Reverend Edwin V. Archbishop of Santa Fe. "Letter to Reverend Augustine Cortez, S.F., Pastor." 20 January 1959

Byrne, Most Reverend Edwin V. Archbishop of Santa Fe. "Letter to Reverend Augustine Cortes, Pastor." 23 January 1959

Byrne, Most Reverend Edwin V. Archbishop of Santa Fe. "Letter to Reverend Sipio A. Salas, Pastor." 19 February 1960

Byrne, Most Reverend Edwin V. "Letter to Reverend Sipio A. Salas, Pastor." 13 June 1959. Print.

Byrne, Most Reverend Edwin V. Archbishop of Santa Fe. "Notification of Boundries." 23 January 1959

Catholic Church Extension Society of the United States of America, President (illegible signature). "Letter to Most Reverend Edwin V. Byrne, D.D." 18 October 1946

Catholic Church Extension Society of the United States of America, President (illegible signature). "Letter to Most Reverend Edwin V. Byrne, D.D." 18 June 1946

Catholic Church Extension Society of the United States of America, President (illegible signature). "Letter to Most Reverend Edwin V. Byrne, D.D." 21 June 1946

Chavez, Domitilia and Pasqual. Personal Interview. 1996

"Christmas Ornaments." *Description of Cynthia Luna's 4th grade Christmas Decorations.* 1997.

Cobos, Rubén. *A Dictionary of New Mexico & Southern Colorado Spanish Revised & Expanded Edition.* Second. Santa Fe, New Mexico: Museum of New Mexico Press, 2003. Print.

Coggiola-Mower, Very Reverend O.A, Chancellor "Letter to Reverend Augustine Cortez, S.F." 7 November 1958

Coggiola-Mower, Very Reverend O.A, Chancellor "Letter to Reverend Augustine Cortez, S.F." 2 June 1958

Delgado, Luis. "Sagrado Corazón de Jesús." *Receipt.* April 24, 1998.

Duran , Gilbert. "Description of Plastering Contract."

"Fire Destroys Old Nambe Church." *Santa Fe New Mexican* [Santa Fe, New Mexico] April 19,1946, n. pag. Print.

Garcia, Andres, Jr. (Andy). "For Sacred Heart Celebration." *Note/Letter Regarding Flag.* 2003.

Garcia, Andres, Sr. Personal Interview. 1994-95.

Gomez, Hilario. "Personal Research, Handwritten Notes."

Gonzales, Benedict J. "Description of Work to Doors." *Receipt for Repair of Doors.*

Gonzales, José. Personal Interview. March 21, 1995

Herrera, Lorenzo. Personal Interview. 1995

"History of Nambe Church Traced Back to Year 1613." *Santa Fe New Mexican* [Santa Fe, New Mexico] 12 April 1946, n. pag. Print.

Hoover, Herbert. The United States of America. President. *Santa Fe 065726.* Washington, DC: US. Government Printing Office, 1932. Print.

Kessell, John. *The Missions of New Mexico Since 1776*. First Edition. Albuquerque, New Mexico: University of New Mexico Press, 1980. Print.

Knoll, John. "Priest simply content to be at Pojoaque." *Santa Fe New Mexican—Pojoaque* [Santa Fe, New Mexico] 24 January 2001, 1-2. Print.

LaPierre Ortiz, Geraldine Ana. "An Ortiz Legacy." Personal Story.

Luján, Carolina M. and Alfredo. "Historia de Nuestro Sagrado Corazón de Jesús." First Edition. Santa Fe, New Mexico: Ortiz Printing, 1997. Print.

Luján, Carolina M. "Letter to Reverend John Cannon, Chancellor."13 January 2011.

Luján, Carolina M. "Letter to Reverend Timothy A. Martinez, Chancellor."14 April 2010.

Luna, Solomon. Personal Interview. 1995

Matic, Cecilia L. "Sofia Madrid Romero." Personal Essay.

Meredith, Grace. Federal Writers' Project. *Nambé Indian Pueblo*. 1936. Print.

Missions of New Mexico. Archives of the Archdiocese of Santa Fe: Print.

Ortiz, Erline. "Letter to Carrie regarding mission in Nambe." 14 June 2012. Print.

Ortiz, Medardo. Personal Interview. 1994 -1995

Prince, L. Bradford. *Spanish Mission Churches of New Mexico*. Cedar Rapids, Iowa: The Torch Press, 1915. Print.

Reinberg, Rt. Reverend F.A. "Letter to Reverend Guadalupe Rivera." 9 May 1964

Romero, Mary and Arturo A. Personal Interview. 1995

Romero, Ramon. Personal Interview. 1995

Romero, Ramoncito. "Letter from Ramoncito Romero."5 September 5, 1994. Print.

St. John, Rt. Reverend Richard R. Catholic Church Extension Society of the United States of America, Vice-President and General Secretary. "Letter to Most Reverend Edwin V. Byrne, D.D." 30 June 1947

Salas, Sipio A. Pastor. "Letter to Most Reverend Edwin V. Byrne, D.D." 8 June 1959

Salas, Reverend Sipio A. "Letter to Most Reverend Edwin V. Byrne, D.D." 17 February 1960

Santillanes, Padre Jose Flavio. "From the Padre's Desk."

Schoeppner, Reverend C.C. "Letter to Most Reverend William D. O'Brian, D.D." 11 October 1946

Schoeppner, Reverend C.C. "Letter to Reverend Gene Salvador, S.F." 1 August 1946

Sena, Claude S. "Letter to Edwin V. Byrne, Archbishop of Santa Fe" 5 August 1960

Senninger, Bernard A. Pastor. "A report on the status of property and finances of Sacred Heart Parisch, Nambé, factors involved in planning, and recommendations." 7 September 1960

Senninger, Bernard A. "Letter to Most Reverend Edwin V. Byrne, D.D." 28 June 1960

Senninger, Bernard A. Pastor. "Letter to Most Reverend Edwin V. Byrne, D.D." 2 August 1960

Senninger, Bernard A. Pastor. "Letter to Most Reverend Edwin V. Byrne, D.D." 6 September 1960

Senninger, Bernard A. Pastor. "Letter to Most Reverend Edwin V. Byrne, D.D." 8 September 1960

Spanish English Translation. <www.spanishdict.com/translation>.

The Tatkoski Studios. "Our Lady of Guadalupe Parish." *Receipt for Repair of Windows.* March 31, 2006.

"Usher Schedule or Sagrado Corazón de Jesús Church, Nambe." 2012.

Velásquez de la Cadena, Mariano, Edward Gray , et al. *Velásquez Spanish English Dictionary.* Chicago New York: Follett Publishing Company, 1974. Print.

Weidner, Urban C. Jr. "Letter to WW. Lamoreux, Contractor." 16 November 1964

Printed in the USA
CPSIA information can be obtained
at www.ICGtesting.com
LVHW081525270823
756447LV00006B/301